The cyclis... legend... **High Li...** ...he Ridge,
Cascadia and *imaginar...* ...acking mo... ...which ...
everything from mo... ...ks, rooftop... ...nd m...
His life is on... ...s, bloody spill... ...s of onli...

It hasn't been a... ...de. Doubt, str... ...e 'what i...
trailblazing... ...hich requires... ...n, fearle... ...g
tec...iques and ...eye for a go... ...era ang... ...as spent his life
pushing the extremes; somehow, he's still around to tell the tale.

In this unflinching memoir of mayhem, Danny shares his anarchic childhood
on the Isle of Skye and early days as a street trials rider, takes us behind
the scenes of his training and videos, and reveals what it takes to go
to the next level – both mentally and physically.

**Join Danny for a nerve-shredding ride.
Just be sure to bring a crash helmet.**

At the Edge

At the Edge

Riding for My Life

DANNY MACASKILL

VIKING
an imprint of
PENGUIN BOOKS

VIKING

UK | USA | Canada | Ireland | Australia
India | New Zealand | South Africa

Viking is part of the Penguin Random House group of companies
whose addresses can be found at global.penguinrandomhouse.com.

First published 2016
001

Copyright © Danny MacAskill, 2016

The moral right of the author has been asserted

Permissions: the lyrics from The Dodos' track 'Fools' thanks to Leafy Green management;
quotes from Channel Four/*Concrete Circus* programme courtesy of director, Mike Christie;
quotes from *The Ridge* from director, Stu Thomson; quotes from Red Bull films
and the Robbie Maddison courtesy of Red Bull

Set in 13.5/16 pt Garamond MT Std
Typeset by Jouve (UK), Milton Keynes
Printed in Great Britain by Clays Ltd, St Ives plc

A CIP catalogue record for this book is available from the British Library

ISBN: 978-0-241-20652-2

www.greenpenguin.co.uk

Contents

CONTENTS

Contents #2

(A.K.A. *Do not try this at home*)

What I do is dangerous, and it's taken years of practice. Unsurprisingly, there have been plenty of bumps and breaks along the way. I'd hate to hear that somebody has been gravely hurt trying to emulate a rider, especially if they've done so after reading this book. Here is a go-to contents list of the injuries I've sustained so far. Should you ever feel the urge to back-flip across a wide gap between two buildings, please read the following pages before getting on your bike . . .

Rider's Speak

A Glossary of Terms

BANGER: The big trick at the end of every video. A showstopper. *The Big Finale.*

BASH RING: A protective steel ring that guards the cog and chain.

DIAL: To do something consistently well.

ENDER: Another word for a Banger.

FAKIE NOSE MANUAL: A reverse wheelie where a rider rolls backwards on their front wheel with the rear wheel off the ground.

FLAIR: A back flip, combined with a 180-degree spin. Often performed in a half-pipe (or, in my case, off a tree); upon landing, the rider should be facing back to where they first started.

FLATLAND: Riding on flat ground. This style often involves spins; the rider might also stand in unorthodox positions on the bike, such as the frame.

FOOTJAM: A stop, executed by 'jamming' the front foot in the front wheel behind the forks. A rider then balances on the front wheel.

FOOTJAM TAILWHIP: A trick where the rider stands on their front wheel while kicking the back end of the bike around. They lift their feet over the bike, replacing them on the pedals once the frame has returned to the starting position.

GAP/GAPPING: A distance or area to be jumped on the bike.

GRIND (RAIL): A trick that involves placing one bike part (the pedals maybe, or the pegs) or a few parts on an obstacle and sliding along it.

LINE: The collective linking of manoeuvres and tricks together in a sequence. It is basically performing two or more tricks in a row over various obstacles.

MANUAL: Coasting on your back wheel, while keeping the front end up without pedalling. You use your body weight and movement to keep the roll going.

PART: Can be a stand-alone riding edit (like *Inspired Bicycles*) or it can be a particular rider's section of a team DVD, or product release (e.g. Alex D.'s part in *Living for the City*/BSD).

RIDER: Somebody who rides – a mountain biker, skateboarder, or BMXer, for example.

ROADIE: A rider who uses a road bike, for example, Sir Bradley.

SKINNY: A narrow line, such as a fallen tree, round railing, or even a spiky fence.

STAIR SET: A set of stairs.

TAILWHIP: The rider hops the bike into the air while kicking the back end out from underneath them and uses their arms to generate enough momentum to rotate the frame 360 degrees.

The rider then catches their pedals with their feet before landing.

TRANSITION: The curve of a ramp.

TYRE-TAP: To stop on the back wheel at the top of an obstacle, such as a wall or rail.

WALLRIDE: To ride at a vertical wall, before jumping on to its face at an angle which allows both wheels to roll along the surface.

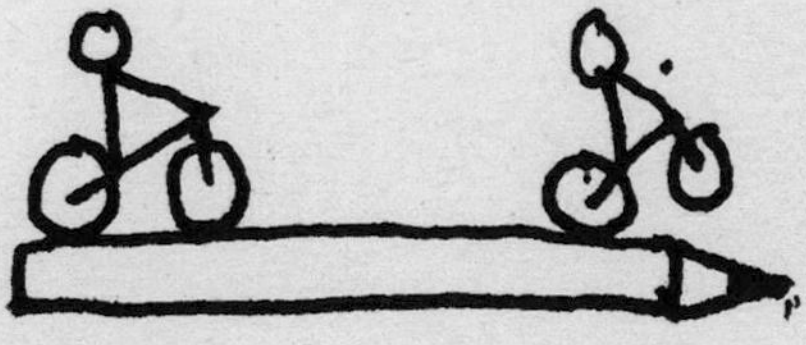

Scene One

FADE IN

(<u>EXT.</u>) The clifftops, Las Palmas de Gran Canaria

Street-trials rider and film-maker Danny MacAskill is preparing for his most dramatic stunt to date: a front flip from a clifftop ramp, a nerve-shredding feat that should propel him past a series of boulders fifty feet below and into the sea — if all goes to plan.

Danny approaches the jump, first by riding the rooftops of Las Palmas under a bright blue sky. He is wearing his Drop And Roll tee and Red Bull helmet. A GoPro has been fixed to the top of it.

Through a POV viewfinder we see him hopping down from a ledge; he drops on to a tower of scaffolding. A makeshift ramp has been built below. He lands at the top, pedalling as fast as he can, the edge rushing into view. The horizon is at the end, plus those rocks and a plunge into the ocean swell . . .

Cascadia, 2015

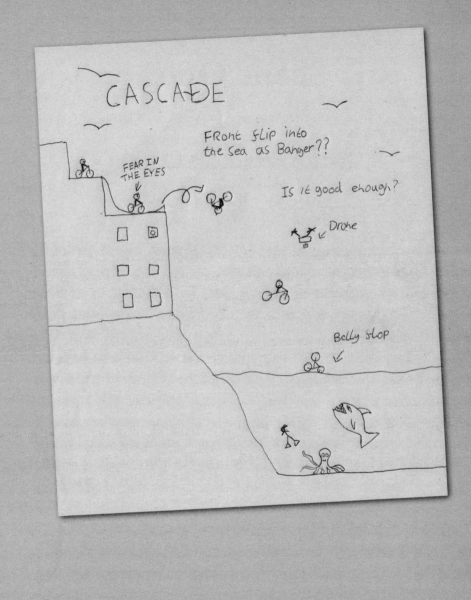

1. Death is Not an Option

Nothing was going to stop me from jumping off the cliff. Not the foaming water; not the jagged rocks that bared their teeth with the retreating tide; not the drop – all fifty feet of it. I was going over the edge, whether my bike liked it or not.

All around me were cameras to record this final banger. One was attached to my helmet, another buzzed overhead on a drone. Each lens was capturing the size and scale of what I was about to attempt: for the spectacular closing shot of a 2015 video we were calling *Cascadia*, I was aiming to race as fast as I could off a ramp. Made from scaffolding, it had been built in a small alley in Las Palmas de Gran Canaria. The end took me off the side of a cliff, plunging me down, down, *down*, in a sheer drop to the sea.

I'd been pretty confident when I'd first suggested the stunt a few weeks earlier, but on the day I began to stress. I worried the speed in my run-up, or lack thereof, wouldn't take me over the rocks at the bottom. In some parts the water was only fifteen feet deep, which made for a landing that was less than ideal in my eyes. Meanwhile, the sea looked turbulent. Huge waves moved below, exposing dozens of crabs clinging to previously unseen boulders. Maybe I needed to rethink my trajectory? Will I have enough speed? At the very least I was facing a painful slap to the body as I broke the surface from a great height. And beyond that? Well, who knows.

That's when it happened – *the click*. After an hour of deliberating, something in my head told me to go. I hit the ramp and pedalled as fast as I could. The buildings whizzed by. The only thing I could hear was the rattling of scaffolding under my tyres.

Clang-a-lang!
Clang-a-lang!
Everything lurched towards me – the sunset, the horizon, the sea. I threw myself over the edge. Wind brushed my face. And then . . .

Nothing.
Only silence.
And relief.

I'm not mad.

I'm sure my YouTube virals might lead you to think differently, but everything I do is planned, calculated; on a bike I know exactly what I'm capable of landing at the top end of my ability, and I only operate within those limits. It might seem like I have a death wish, especially when I'm hurling myself off a cliff face, or across a gap between two tall buildings, but I don't take many risks – not stupid ones, anyway.

Instead, all of my stunts begin with a great deal of preparation, and endless hours of psychological torture: it takes me ages to get my head straight before I'm racing up a ramp and into a bump front flip, or a tyre-tap tailwhip from a huge drop. Most shooting days are spent beating myself up for the fact that I can't just rush headlong into a jump without fretting about it endlessly. I wish I could deal with it better. Sometimes it's a pain in the arse.

Luckily, I don't have any phobias. I'm not afraid of heights, or speed, or even spiders, and I have a weird relationship with pain – it doesn't bother me, which is handy in a lifestyle where spills and face-plants are a constant occupational hazard. But when it comes to streets trials – my style of riding, where I negotiate everyday 'furniture' such as stairways, benches and railings, usually at fairly high speeds, or over great heights – some challenges can put me on edge.

For those of you unsure of what trials riding is about, it started out as a competitive event where a mountain biker had to get up and over obstacles as quickly as they could. The catch? They're not allowed to put their feet on the ground. In a competition setting, this involves a rider negotiating a marked-out route over logs, rocks, walls or old cars. As soon as they enter the start gate, the clock starts ticking. Competitors have to make their way through the section; every time their feet hit the floor it counts as one penalty mark, or 'dab', against them. (The maximum number of dabs a competitor is allowed in one section before being disqualified is five.) Whoever completes the course within the time limit, and with the fewest dabs, is the winner.

Street trials became an extension of that style, but it wasn't competitive. Rather than navigating barricades within a set period, it involves a mountain biker being creative on objects that people use every day. (For example, those bus stops, phone boxes and railings you walk past on the way to work.) In more recent years, these stunts have often been filmed and put out on VHS, or DVD, and now they are placed on to social media, where, if the cyclist has been lucky, they go viral.

Being a street-trials rider can be a risky business. For starters, there are tons of bruises and breaks to endure. I've done it all my life, and made plenty of videos along the way, but the fear of crashing never disappears, especially when it comes to facing the unknown. I once front-flipped off the battlements at Edinburgh Castle – that was pretty nerve-wracking. Another time I leapt from the top of an abandoned slaughterhouse in a derelict Argentinian town: on one side was a thirteen-foot drop on to an unstable ceiling (which was the start of my line on this building); on the other an exposed drop of forty feet on to slabs of broken concrete. The stress kicked in for that one, too. And then there was the time I rode across the spiky fence, where one slip could have caused a nasty injury to my nether regions.

When forcing myself to execute a stunt, I have to flick

what I call the 'Commitment Switch' – a trigger that takes me from an anxious state into a more positive mood, but to get there I can cruise around in circles for hours. I even talk to myself, because it's such a stressful experience, especially when I'm standing on a ledge that's forty or fifty feet above ground, or preparing to flip over an obstacle where landing badly might have serious consequences. I doubt myself. Worry tends to creep in. But I have my goal in mind, I flick the switch and get it done.

As I place my feet on to the pedals I do sometimes feel a surge of energy. Everything around me seems to melt away in that moment – the wind, the noise, the fear, those cameras. I grow completely focused on what I have to do, and how I have to do it. Usually, it's a trick I've visualized hundreds of times beforehand. I just need to see it through to the end, hopefully without crashing.

People always ask me how it feels to land a great jump or a banger. It's often just a sense of relief. There's no adrenaline. There's no exhilaration. It's as if I'm going through the motions of what I'd already figured out. The next thing I know, I've generally landed at the bottom in one piece. A feeling of satisfaction kicks in, but it's fleeting. Once I've checked it looks right on camera, then I can begin to unwind . . . maybe even celebrate.

Sometimes it doesn't go to plan – I fall, or land badly – but even in those moments it seems better than looking over the handlebars and wondering, What if? When wiping out, I can at least feel what I have to do to get it right.

8

That makes it easier to go back up there and do it all over again – to get it dialled – because I know what's over the other side.

To a lot of people, my stunts might look a little unwise, or even life-threatening, but I don't think that way. I'm in control, and I'm probably more stable on two wheels than I am on two feet. In *Cascadia*, I cut about on roofs and balconies that were a foot or two wide. On one side was a flat surface – *safety*; on the other a drop of several storeys – *injury, very serious injury*. That height alone would be enough to give most people nightmares, but I was perfectly happy riding across and gapping from edge to edge. It didn't feel that dangerous. I've done lines like that (at street level) so many times that, even if I were to lose my balance, I knew I could fall in such a way that I wouldn't injure myself. I can shift my weight in a split second to land building-side rather than rag-dolling to the pavement below.

Most of the time I put those thoughts to the back of my mind and rethink where I am. Rather than seeing the narrow ledge and the huge drop below me, I imagine I'm back in my garden as a kid, cycling along the thin path that used to run from one end of the lawn to the other. I would cycle up and down that line, over and over, without ever coming off. Seeing myself back there often helps me to forget the consequence of falling because, well . . . *I'm not falling.*

Of course, something disastrous *could* happen. My bike might have a mechanical failure which throws me off at the worst possible moment, but overall, I'm confident. I've checked my equipment and I'm comfortable in what I'm doing. After that, I have to keep my concentration and, psychologically, I'm a calculating person. I don't have the wiring in my head to be entirely reckless or careless, and I have enough fear not to want to risk my life for the sake of landing a stunt that's out of my comfort zone.

Given all that, you might wonder what the hell drives me to try all this stuff. Well, I have a creative mind, and I love pushing myself. Most of all, I love trials. I have done ever since I was a little boy. At first it was a cool way to throw myself about when I was growing up. Later, as I fell more into Scotland's riding scene, it became an obsession. By the time I got to making my first proper videos, with some seriously talented directors, it became a way of expressing myself, and I became more and more imaginative, making exciting parts in a style that hadn't been done before.

That work has taken me beyond the core mountain-bike world and into the mainstream, and I've appeared in TV documentaries, Hollywood movies and adverts. I have been asked to join a Korean circus. A US chat-show host even wanted me to dress up as a woman and race through Chicago. (I turned that one down, by the way. High heels aren't my thing.) As the hits on YouTube went into tens of millions, sponsorship deals with the likes of Red Bull came around. But all I've ever wanted is to mess about on my bike. It's where I'm happiest and have the most fun. Learning new tricks and pushing trials forward with my films – where I can negotiate challenging obstacles, or create interesting studio environments — is what I'm all about. The rest is a sideshow.

Not everyone sees it my way, though. I've released a few films now and, after every one, somebody will take issue with the riding. People will post on YouTube that I've been reckless. They'll tell me that I'm playing with my life. But nine times out of ten, the small amount of folk making those comments haven't been riding trials for nineteen years. Anyway, I'm not that bothered what people say, though I'd rather they were taking the internet clips for what they're meant to be: creative projects that showcase trials in a new and exciting way.

Luckily, there's been lots of support for my stuff so far, which is cool because I want to ride hard and keep making videos I love for as long as I can. That's why I won't take stupid risks. I'm not crazy; I want to keep going, and a healthy fear of crashing isn't going to stop me from fulfilling my ambitions.

It hasn't stopped me so far . . .

Scene Two

FADE IN

(EXT.) Danny's house

The camera is positioned on the edge of Loch
Dunvegan on the Isle of Skye, Scotland. In the
distance is a house, sitting on the edge of the
water. We zoom in through the window of a
downstairs bedroom. A sticker bearing the
Imaginate logo (with the tagline 'Enter Danny's
Mind') has been stuck to the glass.

(INT.) Young Danny's bedroom

Flashback: An eight-year-old Danny is playing.
He sits on the floor, cross-legged. Around him are
plastic soldiers, a model Formula 1 racing car,
brightly coloured rubber balls and one Hot
Wheels-style loop-the-loop track. He's building
an imaginary trials course from his toys.
'Runaway' by Houston bleeds out from a radio. We
focus on Danny's eyes as he manoeuvres a plastic
bike, complete with rider, across the course.

Real time: Cut to the 'modern-day Danny' in
the studio, preparing to race across a
reconstructed, super-sized version of his
childhood bedroom . . .

Imaginate, 2013

2. Way Back Home

As a wee kid, I was impossible to control.

I loved taking risks, and as soon as my mum, Anne, had unleashed me into the wild from the age of seven, I spent all my time out in the woods with my mates, hacking down trees, making bonfires and pushing boulders over cliff edges. I'd sneak away to places where nobody could see the results of my destruction. Hours later, I'd return home sheepishly – maybe with singed hair, a few scrapes and bruises, or in pain from a nail going through my foot. I knew that Mum was going to be mad because I'd torn my fourth pair of trousers that month. To some, my behaviour would have been considered a bit wild, nuts even. My antics might have got me into serious trouble in Glasgow or London. Luckily (for the Crown Prosecution Service, anyway), I was raised in Dunvegan, on Scotland's Isle of Skye. I was free to run feral.

In reality, the chaos that trailed me was never anything more than the fallout to some over-enthusiastic high-jinx, and there was rarely panic from my parents. Whenever I flew through the front door, blood dripping from a cut head, or a second-degree burn to my hands, Mum would fix me with a stern look. 'Well, that was a bit stupid, wasn't it, Daniel?' she'd say, tutting at the latest injury. I'd rarely receive any sympathy. Sometimes I was given a treat to keep me occupied as they decided whether to drive me forty miles to the local hospital, but only if I had got myself into a bad state.

Around the age of eight I found an old metal plough attached to a wall outside the museum run by my dad, Peter (we'll get on to that in a bit). It must have weighed six hundred pounds. At one end was a horribly angled rusty handle with razor-sharp edges. I saw it as a climbing frame and decided it would be a good idea to swing from the end. As I jumped up and made a grab for a handhold, the plough toppled down on top of me, its handle scything through the skin on the back of my head. It *stung*. Blood was running down my neck.

Not that I was too bothered. I walked back into the house, looking to patch myself up, but Mum realized I was in trouble. There was nothing in the way of panic, though. Instead, she inspected the cut, reaching into the cupboard for a packet of chocolate buttons, the one thing she knew that might keep me from fidgeting. Once it was decided that, aye, the cut wasn't as bad as it looked, I was bandaged up and told not to do it again. But, really, it was a miracle that the plough hadn't lopped my head off.

Don't get me wrong: Mum was strict. She wasn't one for letting me get away with just anything, particularly if it involved tormenting my younger sister, which was another of my favourite pastimes. Looking back, this is the only aspect of my childhood where I feel any kind of remorse, but I tell myself it is part of who she is today. If I misbehaved, some form of punishment would follow soon after, and a lot of my friends were quite scared of her, especially if she was really 'ticked off' with me. I was, too. If ever I wanted to go off to a friend's house, or into the woods to play, I'd always ask my dad. He was easier to persuade. When it came to the injuries, Mum later told me that she'd been happy to adapt to my mischief, rather than wrapping me up in cotton wool. On her part, there had been no real master plan to toughen me up, but Dad often looked worried whenever I stumbled through the door like a Tasmanian Devil. I think it might have stressed him out a little.

My thing was destruction, and I was into it in a big way. I never did anything to other people's property; I wasn't a vandal or malicious. But there was something indescribably satisfying about seeing a tree branch snap, or an old wall collapse in the middle of nowhere. Whenever teachers asked me what I'd like to be when I was older, I'd tell them, 'Demolition expert.' I dreamed of blowing up buildings for a living, and practising my art on nature, often with abandoned household objects, became an all-consuming hobby. I'd smuggle my dad's saws into Dunvegan Primary School so I could hack at tree limbs at lunch, and when I discovered Granddad's old Second World War machete in a shed, it became a vital tool for my den-building projects in the nearby woods.

One day, there was a bit of a drama when I pulled out the blade in class. My big reveal took place during an amateur Punch & Judy performance that was visiting the school, which wasn't the best idea. Everybody froze. Even Punch stopped battering Judy for five seconds – he'd been completely upstaged by a junior hell-raiser. My teacher took one look at me as if to say, What the heck?, and quickly confiscated the knife, handing it back to my parents after school, probably with some stern advice about how to control their machete-wielding maniac of a son.

I loved growing up in Dunvegan. Skye is a remote spot, one of the most northerly islands within the Inner Hebrides; Dunvegan is a small fishing village with a population of maybe three hundred and fifty people. Set on the loch, it was pretty idyllic. Summer tourists were drawn to Dunvegan Castle and the hills called MacLeod's Tables. I could even see the Black Cuillins from the bottom of my road, a range of mountains topped by the Inaccessible Pinnacle, a slice of rock only five hundred feet across at its longest edge. Its rugged terrain would later become the location for one of my most popular videos, *The Ridge*, though my earlier adventures there were pretty tame. We might swim in the 'Fairy Pools' at the bottom, but any designs on scaling the daunting peaks were a long way off.

The main part of town had a couple of pubs, a police station, some shops and a small hotel. And while this was hardly a suburban high street, it was Skye's north-western hub – its Times Square or Sunset Boulevard. Often, folk would drive twelve miles to visit, grabbing their groceries and newspapers from the local store before heading straight back home. To some people on the island, if you lived in our village you were considered to be a 'city slicker'.

Dunvegan was a natural assault course. There was fun to be had away from the shops – in the woods, on the beach and along the crags. Adventurous kids like me thrived there. I became obsessed with jumping off the highest edges I could find, even as a toddler. At my house, Tigh na Bruaich – House in the Hill – there was a giant play-pen in the garden. Made up of rope swings, climbing frames and a tree house built from old torpedo storage cases that Dad had found God knows where, it, too, became an obstacle course, and at the age of four I'd be climbing into the branches and launching myself out with a crash.

That streak never left me, and at one of my birthday parties, when I was around nine, I broke up some old netting from a football goal. We strung it up in the trees like a hammock and all the kids took turns jumping on to the rope canopy. Hurling myself through the air became such a buzz that I made it my mission to expand the landing zone and, in school, I'd sketch out construction blueprints for the garden and dream up bigger and bolder leaps with my friends so I could extend the flying distances across the nets.

Fortunately, there was plenty of detritus for me to build with. On weekends, I'd head down to the beach with friends, gapping from rock pool to rock pool, looking for washed-up fishing net and snagged pieces of wood. We'd find debris, long wooden poles for example. To most people this stuff was rubbish, but to us it was ideal bonfire material. Lengths of tough rope were perfect for the garden, but moving that stuff was a mission. A huge net could weigh a ton, and we'd spend whole weekends dragging it as far as we could (sometimes up to four miles), before stashing it somewhere safe. The next weekend we'd go back again, and pull it even further. As soon as we were close enough to the road, Dad would dump it into the back of his pick-up truck and drive us back to the house.

At home, I'd raid Mum's kitchen drawers for tools, climbing around the netting, usually having borrowed her carving knife so I could hack at any loose rope. To check the blade, I would first carve an edge across the bookcases and doors in the house. Once satisfied, I'd hack at the garden play-nets and climb among the trees, the knife gripped between my teeth like a delinquent Jack Sparrow. By the time it was dark, the knife would be abandoned in the garden.

Dinner would come around soon after, which was when Mum started rummaging for her best blades. If she couldn't find any in the kitchen, she'd know I was to blame. A drawer would slam. She would fix a stern glare upon me.

'Daniel, bring back my knives or I'll shoot the boots off you!'

Reluctantly, I'd scale the nets, usually in the pouring rain and cold, retrieving her best kitchen equipment, which had been stabbed into the bark of a tree.

I was a bit of a brat. Most of the time, my mischief involved matches, and I'd build big bonfires in the garden, raiding

Dad's sheds for tins of petrol, or anything else that might catch alight. I'd pour the liquid on to a mountain of wood and peat, staring as it went up in flames. I loved explosions, too. Sometimes the blazes at home became so big that the Dunvegan sky would resemble a war zone, with thick, black smoke drifting out across the loch from our backyard, engulfing the village.

Mum and Dad soon got wind that I was a pyromaniac-in-waiting and hid the matches. Any flammable liquids that might have been lying around the house were stashed away. But that wasn't going to stop me. I was crafty, and able to pop into the local shop to buy boxes of Swan Vestas. Meanwhile, nobody ever batted an eyelid at the eight-year-old in the garage, on an errand, picking up cans of lawnmower petrol 'for Dad'.

I got burned a few times. I set both my legs ablaze, my arms, too, and it was a miracle that I didn't get severely injured. But I came pretty close. I learned that jerry cans of petrol and a lit match could be a dangerous combination – the burning liquid sometimes came back at me as I ran away. My friends and I also developed a fascination with melting lead. A batch we'd been cooking one time was knocked over, and a drop of molten goo landed on my hand with a sizzle. I stood there watching as it seemed to melt into my skin. I reckon it might still be in my system, along with a metal plate and the screws bolting my collarbone together after a crash I had in my twenties. I'm a nightmare at airport security.

My passion around the age of eight was rolling boulders from the cliffs, and I loved taking missions into MacLeod's

Tables with a group of schoolmates. On our way to the top we'd carry huge pinch bars – six-foot-long rods of iron – so we could shift heavy rocks off the peaks. Whatever the weather, we'd be playing on those hills; if it was blowing a hoolie with icy, stinging sheets of rain hammering our faces, I'd put on my yellow wellies (safety first), and head out with the aim of nudging the biggest boulder I could find off the crag's edge and into the sea below. Some of the stones were massive – much bigger than me – and so I'd climb on top to get the right amount of leverage, jamming a pinch bar underneath. For safety, I'd tie myself to one end of a rope while some mates held the other end. I hoped the makeshift harness would stop me from falling off the edge. Once the rock started to move, I'd spring away to avoid tumbling to my doom.

I've no idea where the high-jinx came from. Mum was a clerk for a local building firm, and Dad curated the Giant MacAskill Museum in Dunvegan, a collection dedicated to our famous family relative, Angus MacAskill. According to legend, he stood at seven foot nine inches in height, and the *Guinness Book of World Records* made him the 'tallest-ever non-pathological giant'. He was also built like a brick outhouse and had the biggest chest of any 'non-obese man', measuring an impressive eighty inches.

Unsurprisingly, Angus became a bit of a local hero on the Isle of Berneray, where he lived for a while during the early nineteenth century. Once word got out that he could carry a three-hundred-pound barrel of port under each arm without breaking sweat, P. T. Barnum's world-famous circus came calling. Angus was soon being paid to travel around America, where he was challenged to plenty of brawls (most of which he probably won) and performed feats of incredible strength. Apparently, he could lift a fully grown horse over a four-foot fence. Fascinated by these stories, Dad opened the museum in 1989, and it became a curiosity on Skye. Tourists often stopped by. Everyone wanted to hear about Angus's life. When I was little, I told the other kids in school that there had been a monster in my family.

The more I get into making videos and coming up with stunts today, like throwing myself from a cliff into the sea on my bike, or gapping off one rooftop to another, the more I've realized that Dad's creative spirit is probably at the heart of a lot of it. Curating a museum about a family giant is a pretty crazy idea when you think about it, but he saw an opportunity and thought it would be an interesting thing to do. When it comes to business, Dad's not gone about his work in a predictable way. I seem to have followed him by living a life less ordinary, too.

Compared to Angus, the rest of our family were rather short. I was born on 23 December 1985. I have one sister, Margaret Ishbel, two years my junior, two stepbrothers, Ewen and Robin, and two stepsisters, Mary and Muriel. Dad had been married previously, and my half-siblings were all a little older than me, so we never actually lived in the same home. They were raised just across the water from myself and Margaret Ishbel in a place called Borreraig, and that was probably just as well. Ewen was into his motorcycles and once broke his back and legs in a horrible accident.

Robin is an excellent kite surfer; Mary broke her arm while messing around with some cars in a nearby field with my brothers. Not one to shy away from a drama, Margaret Ishbel has always been quite the character and is affectionately known on the island as 'Maggie Mayhem'. I guess they had a similar attitude to me as kids: the MacAskill family lived out in the sticks and had to make their own fun.

I don't know how Mum put up with the trouble I caused. It must have given her nightmares. But, miraculously, I was never hospitalized. Sure, there were cuts, and some bumps to the head, but for a long while I was convinced I'd been made from rubber, because nothing ever got broken. My first memorably painful encounter happened when I collided with a tower of chairs while running down a school corridor. The impact cracked a few ribs. But most of the time I could fall off a high wall and jump right up again. Pain and injury didn't seem to bother me.

One time in my garden, I tumbled out of a tree. I was about twenty feet up, and I landed heavily on my back; a bump to the head knocked me clean out. God knows how long I stayed like that, unconscious on the lawn but, when I came round, I crawled towards the house for help before passing out again in the porch. Weirdly, it took me next to no time to pull myself together. I certainly didn't want to go to the doctor's, and the next day I was up in the trees, figuring out crazy new ways of jumping into the nets. In a funny way, I was preparing myself for a life of trying not to hurt myself. (While looking to the outside world like I really wanted to.)

Scene Three

<u>FADE IN</u>

(<u>EXT.</u>) Loch Dunvegan

A motorhome carrying Danny and his bike winds through the Scottish Highlands. He's driving along the A850, towards Dunvegan.

We cut to a series of tricks in a variety of local locations: Danny gaps walls between dams and bridges; he rides railings outside the local police station; in Dunvegan's campsite, he performs a 360-degree footjam tailwhip on top of his camper van. A bunny-hop front flip is executed from a water tank overlooking Dunvegan and MacLeod's Tables. In this scene, Danny has returned home to nail the tricks he learned as a boy.

Way Back Home, 2010

3. Son of Anarchy

My first bike was a beast, a black-and-red kiddies' Raleigh that my dad found in a skip. I was four when it was brought home and tuned up. Dad cleaned off the rust as best he could before handing it over as a present. Whoever had thrown it away hadn't thought to include the stabilizers, so my early adventures began with a helpful push from Mum or Dad, before I inevitably veered off, ploughed into a wall or ended face down on the pavement.

I soon got the hang of it, and crashes never put me off. I was riding, and I loved it. Having already thrown myself around in the garden, I figured that cruising about on two wheels was just another way to have fun. Even on that little Raleigh I'd try tricks on the grass; once I'd mastered cycling from point A to point B, I upgraded to jumping off the patio steps, which were about a foot high; I got used to flying off tree roots and skidding by the poppies at the end of the lawn. It wasn't long before I was building small jumps on the paths.*

* Just so you know, I've always worn a helmet. From the moment I was able to burn about the place on my Raleigh, I had one on my head. Luckily,

The bike even came in handy when I started at Dun-vegan Primary. We lived three quarters of a mile away from the school, and the roads were nowhere near as gnarly as they are in a big city, so from the age of seven I was often allowed to travel in on my own. Cycling along those pavements was a dream, and the mornings were always calm, but once it came to home time the kids would line up and race through the streets – and it was brilliant. One afternoon some of the older lads taught me how to ride with no hands. After that I would tear about with my arms in the air, flying down the school brae and on to the main road. The race home was a free-for-all.

Thinking about it, the route to my front door was like a pump track, and the more I did it, the more I got to learn the best obstacles along the way. I knew which kerbs were going to give me air if I hit them fast enough; I'd gone over some patches of grass so often that they had been sculpted into little jumps for me to kick off – there was a great one by the petrol station. I soon became inseparable from the Raleigh and, once I'd got a bit older, I was able to travel further afield, visiting friends who lived a few miles away. I also started trying new tricks. Riding with no hands was just the begin-ning, and it wasn't long before I'd learned how to wheelie along the street. Nailing it for the first time was awesome, and I'd spend ages in the local car park, gliding along on my back wheel, using the painted strips that had been marked

they've never been out of fashion in trials, and they've definitely saved me a few times, though I've split a couple during tricks and lines.

out for cars as challenges. At first I could manage one space, then two; making it to three was a proper benchmark.

The first trick I perfected was the snake skid. I would pedal as fast as I could, then slam on the brakes before side-winding across the ground like an adder. The pavements in front of my house were run-down, covered with dirt and gravelly; I'd burn across them, my back wheel flaring out behind me, the Raleigh's tyres carving back and forth across the path. I was always riding hard, and by the time I'd made it to the age of ten – somehow alive, and in one piece – that little kids' cycle was in bits. Over the years, all my bikes took a real beating. I was probably the most regular customer in Island Cycles, the local store.

I eventually took up another Raleigh, the Burner, an old-school BMX which had been handed down by a mate. It was too small for me, but I saw that as a good thing. It meant I could throw it around quite easily, much more than I'd be able to on a bike that was suitably sized for my age, and it wasn't long before I was clambering on top of the local bottle bank. Nobody in the village had jumped down from it before. Even my friends' older brothers hadn't risked cycling across it, because the drop was six feet.

Not me. One evening, while messing around with my mate Kenneth, I decided to take a run at it. I knew the jump was within my range, but I guessed there was a 50 per cent chance that I might nose dive, head first, off the edge. But as I climbed to the top and Kenneth passed the Burner up, I reassured myself: I had already jumped four feet on the Burner, why couldn't I do six?

On reflection, those two extra feet looked a heck of a lot riskier, and the odds on a successful landing lengthened big-time. I glanced at Kenneth. Worry was etched into his face.

'Are you sure about this, Danny?' he said. The poor kid was steeling himself for a 999 call.

I nodded, though I wasn't really sure. It might have been the first time I'd had to wrestle with my fear a little, even though I'd jumped greater distances without the bike: I would happily leap ten feet out of a tree and tumble to the ground – no problem. The bottle bank was different, probably because riding it was a mythical benchmark in Dunvegan.

Hmm, I thought. I'm not quite sure how this is gonna work out . . .

I crept forward, lifted my front wheel, and suddenly felt the lurch of gravity as I sailed off the edge. The pavement loomed up in a blur and, in that split second, my right foot slipped off the pedal, causing me to wobble. Somehow, I retained control, and my tyres hit the concrete with a crunch. I cruised away with a banging heart; a crazy buzz. I was in one piece and my rep on the island had just grown a little. On two wheels, I was fast becoming the local menace.

When I was eleven, my aunts Jean and Sarah gave me a Kona Fire Mountain as a birthday present, a decent mountain bike, and that marked my first steps towards taking riding seriously. I fixated on it. I read cycling magazines and watched videos; I talked about new equipment and the best riders with my mates, all the while obsessing over parts and tricks. I used my Kona for everything – missions into the woods, long trips across the hills and tricks around the village. I would build bigger and better jumps in the garden and try to throw myself over Dad's lawnmower. It had big saw blades attached to the front, and one slip could have resulted in a pretty messy trip to the hospital. I wasn't emulating anyone, like the motorcycle rider Evel Knievel. I was just getting a kick from trying out new stunts.

Discovering trials was a game-changer. The first video I saw was *Chainspotting*, the 1997 Mountain Biking UK movie, which showcased the scene's top riders. Martyn Ashton was on there; Martin Hawyes, Hans Rey, too. Each of them did tricks over bollards and benches. One of them even dropped off a ten-foot-high roof. I knew from the kids at school that riders were performing tricks of that style on a BMX, but seeing it done with a mountain bike was all new. It was pretty inspirational. I'd already been attempting that style myself, creating stunts from my own imagination. Seeing other people doing it, I was mesmerized.

To my mind, *Chainspotting* took trials to the next level. The style being broken out by Martyn Ashton and Martin Hawyes, as well as cycling legend Hans Rey, was a spin-off from the competition format, and was more focused on tricks. Everything was in an urban setting and involved a cyclist negotiating bus stops and railings in car parks and on high streets. It was stuff I could aspire to ride and the aesthetic was appealing. I loved jumping around in the nets at home. I liked climbing trees. I also liked beachcombing for materials that could be added to my home-made assault course, and that process had often involved me hopping from rock pool to rock pool, calculating the space between each leap. Trials required a similar thought process. It involved assessing distances and approach lines. In a way, it was puzzle-solving. But instead of navigating their way around a beach or scrambling over rocks, Martyn, Martin and Hans were hopping across a water tank on two wheels or 360ing off a high wall.

The tricks Martyn and Hans were doing were way more appealing than any of the stunts being pulled off in skateboarding. Dunvegan's terrain was just too rough for that. But on a mountain bike I could be more versatile, and I was able to ride all the surfaces around town, whatever the conditions. After *Chainspotting*, my imagination ran wild. I began cutting around the village in an inspired mood, practising my wheelies, skids, and jumping off walls and flowerbed baskets. (But I never damaged the plants – honest.)

I quickly got a rep as the local ASBO-in-waiting, which was unsurprising when you think of the neighbourhood. There wasn't a lot of crime in Dunvegan; I was probably the closest our police station had ever got to a *Crimewatch*-style fugitive, and I was forever getting under the feet of people walking along the main road. Because I lived in the centre of town, I was a nuisance from the minute I rode out the front door. Folk started to grumble, and not just in the summer when I was out and about during the holidays, but in the winter, too.

Skye isn't blessed with easy weather. Most of the time it's raining and freezing cold, and that's in July. Come the depths of January, when the wind is blowing across the water, it was impossible to cut around on the streets, so I'd head for a little shopping centre called Kinloch instead (or as it was known to us, the Gun Shop). Located on the main road that led to Dunvegan Castle, it had been built with a roof to protect shoppers from the rain. It was also illuminated in the evening, and there were several steps and flowerbeds for me to practise on – it was perfect! The Gun Shop soon became my regular hangout, and it wasn't long before the square-edged brick walls had been rounded off with my bash-ring. Those times were vital in developing my style. I owe a lot to that place.

But the Gun Shop didn't love me back. There were complaints, and the local cop, PC Duncan Carmichael, quickly became the Special Agent Hank Schrader to my Walter White. He loved catching me out, even though my riding was pretty inoffensive – well, most of the time. Sure, I'd be pulling wheelies down the road, and sometimes I wouldn't use any lights, but it wasn't like I was acting crazy. I'd never dart in front of a moving car, or drop off a bus stop as a bunch of terrified pensioners cowered for safety underneath. On the flipside, I knew that what I was doing was enough to land me in hot water, but I persevered because I didn't have anything else to do. It wasn't like there was a PlayStation or computer in the house. I didn't watch much TV. Riding was my main outlet, and I loved it. So at seven or eight o'clock in the evening, every day, I'd jump from one wall to another on my Kona Fire Mountain in the Gun Shop, the howling wind and rain swirling about outside.

PC Carmichael didn't see it my way. He was forever dragging me home, complaining to my parents about how I was becoming a public issue, which seemed a bit extreme. I wasn't exactly the model kid, but I hadn't been boozing on street corners until 2 a.m. either. Still, it didn't take long for my parents to start losing their rag.

'We'll take that bicycle from you!' yelled Mum one night.

She understood my love of messing around outdoors, but I was becoming a royal pain in the arse. I was just as bad in class, where I was being called out as a trouble magnet, especially once I'd started at Portree High School, a secondary school forty-five minutes outside Dunvegan. I wasn't a horrible kid; I wasn't a bully and I was never one for fighting as I got into my teens, but around the age of thirteen, I became disruptive. I had way too much energy for my own good, and I had plenty of mates who were more than happy to encourage my reckless streak.

I was the smallest in my school year, and I became a crash-test dummy. My friends would concoct a plan – a jump or a prank – and I'd be called in as the stuntman. The flaws became apparent only once I'd landed in a crumpled heap, or if I'd been hauled off to the headmaster's office. Meanwhile, my grades were hit and miss. I was OK at practical subjects like craft and design and physics, but I struggled with anything that involved writing, like English or history. I was later diagnosed with dyslexia, which meant that I found reading much harder than most kids. My attention could wander quite quickly, and I'd usually catch myself daydreaming in lessons, fantasizing about new tricks or riding a fresh line. Forget the textbooks: my focus was all about the wall or bench outside the classroom window.

In the end, a lack of discipline resulted in my suspension, and the final straw arrived when I was busted for skelping the back of the school bus driver's head with a Malteser. He was taking us home one afternoon and, as everybody began messing about, I pinged a chocolate ball against his head. It was a great shot, but as it struck his skull with a dull pop I knew I'd blown it. There was a shout. The driver's back arched. His foot slammed hard on the brakes.

'Right! I'm taking you lot to the police!' he yelled.

I thought he was kidding – we all did. The bus was miles from school. But we were wrong. The driver turned around and drove all the way to Portree police station. Even then, nobody took the threat too seriously. That changed when an officer came on board and ordered us to spill. I felt sick. I was convinced somebody would bust me, but everybody stuck to the Code of the Playground; nobody squealed and the bus eventually dropped us home. However, once we'd all been threatened with a group detention by the school a few days later, I 'fessed up and was suspended. The mood at home was bad. I was temporarily out of classes, my grades were poor and the police were complaining about my late-night activities. Talk about making myself exceedingly unpopular. And then, in a cruel twist of fate, PC Carmichael confiscated my trials bike.

It was a bit over the top. The incident had happened on a summer's evening when some friends and me had found an abandoned teddy by a rubbish bin. The roads were dead, so I placed the toy in the middle of the street and tried to bunny-hop over it. Suddenly, I heard a siren. There were some flashing lights, too. Within seconds, the place resembled the scene of a drugs bust. PC Carmichael, my friend from the blues and twos, was screeching towards us in his patrol car. He'd been parked down the road and was watching as the whole sketch unfolded.

'Quick! Run!' somebody shouted. Everyone scattered – some kids jumped into the bushes; others ran for a nearby car park; I hid behind the bottle bank. When I clocked PC Carmichael creeping around a parked school bus, I tried to make a bolt for it, but he was on me in a flash, grabbing the bike and throwing it against a wall. He even read me my rights.

'Daniel MacAskill, I'm arresting you for dangerous cycling,' he raged. 'Anything you say may be used against you in a court of law . . . '

It was pure madness. I just remember thinking, I'm on my bicycle – I'm not smashing somebody's windows, or rolling about hammered.

I was hauled off home and told that my bike was being confiscated by the police for the rest of the summer. Worse, I had to face a Children's Panel – a court system for kids – where I was charged. It was pretty scary. As my 'crimes' were read out, I had visions of ending up in a juvenile detention centre, though, luckily, it didn't come to that. Instead, I was let off with a warning. I had no bike, way too much energy, and a whole holiday to kill. For the rest of the summer I'd have to find other destructive and mischievous ways of filling my time, so I jumped around in the nets, started huge blazes and fired stones from my catapult at PC Carmichael's house.

Frustration wasn't the half of it.

Scene Four

(<u>EXT.</u>) Cape Town, South Africa

A bright, sunny day. Danny is riding along an
empty city street. One or two pedestrians walk
past, oblivious as to what might happen next.
Moments later we see him wheeling along a
pedestrianized area. Next he rides a pavement
before jumping up a flight of steps and on to a
series of bicycle railings, hopping across them
on his back wheel. As he hits the final edge,
Danny gaps across to a wall, rides to the ends
before pulling a 360 tailwhip drop to the
sidewalk. The streets of Cape Town have been
transformed into a trials course.

Danny MacAskill Plays Cape Town, 2011

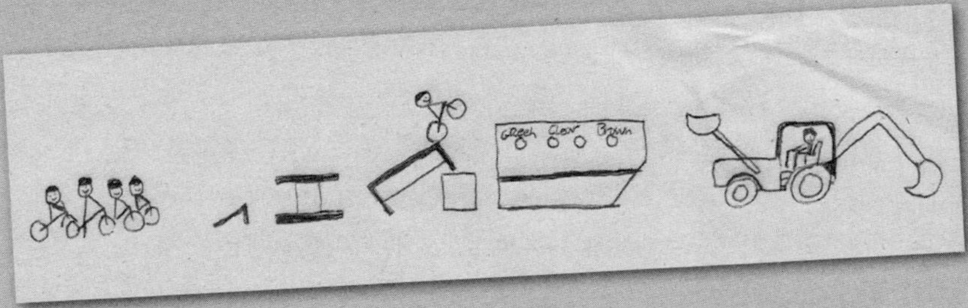
Green
Clear
Brown

4. Ken and the Inverness Gang

A little trials scene had kicked up in Dunvegan. There was my cousin, Donnie McPhee, who lived in Broadford – a town on the south of the island – and me. We were joined by a couple of mates, Jamie Stewart and Alex Kozikowski, and sometimes Donnie would visit after school. Whenever we went riding we would push each other to bigger and better tricks. Meanwhile, Portree High became a hub for kids who were mad into bikes, because there was nowhere else for them to meet. Often, we'd hang out after class and chat about tricks and new frames, the stuff we'd seen in magazines.

Good news: after the summer holidays, my glorious bike was back, reclaimed from PC Carmichael, and I was soon developing the art of 180s and 360s in the Gun Shop, skidding around under streetlights. I easily conquered all the benches and walls in the village, and there was nothing new to challenge my techniques. Dunvegan's limited riding terrain also meant that few riders went there, so there wasn't a more experienced cyclist in town to influence me. I was developing without rules. The only limit to what I could try was my imagination, and that was brimming with plans.

My friends and I worked on street tricks that we had seen on our beloved *Chainspotting*; we used skills that were usually applied to comp trials, but in a quiet high street. I loved testing myself. When I managed twenty back-hops one day, I thought, I've done it! When I heard that Donnie had notched up twenty-four in Broadford, I respected his effort . . . but I had to beat it! That was a strange sensation for me. I wasn't a competitive kid. I didn't enjoy team sports, like football or shinty, the aggressive style of hockey played in school, I was much more focused on individual pursuits. I channelled my energy into the bike, which I loved. It meant everything to me.

Donnie, Jamie, Alex and myself became super-geeky about our bikes. I was immersed in the culture of riding and fantasized about improving my Kona Fire Mountain with new parts. It was probably only natural that I would soon fancy the life of a cycle mechanic and, after months, maybe years, of flicking through the pages of magazines, I figured, Well, I love all the high-end gear, it would be great to put other people's bikes together for them. Turning my passion into a vocation seemed like a win-win, and it became my main aspiration in and outside of school. I told teachers I wanted to focus on a practical trade. At home, I loved tuning up my bike and, whenever a new magazine came out, I drooled over the latest flashy equipment.

I was upgrading my own gear, too. When I later snapped

the front end off my previously confiscated bike, I asked for a Pashley, as ridden by the trials-riding Tongue brothers, Matt and Eddie. I'd seen it advertised in *Mountain Biking UK*, and any kid who knew their cycles understood that the Pashley had been designed with agility in mind. It was also built to withstand the toughest of conditions. The Pashley was perfect for a rider of my ambitions and imagination. Their TV-series 26Mhz trials frame came in baby blue and was constructed with paper-thin Reynolds 853 tubes. In a side note: when motorcycle racer Guy Martin broke the land speed record on a mountain bike in 2015 he used a Reynolds 853 steel frame. It was an impressive piece of kit. And I wouldn't have had the chance to ride one if it hadn't been for my generous grandma buying it for me.

With a serious bike to ride on, I became even more fascinated by trials, though keeping up with the latest developments wasn't easy. When I was fifteen, it was the year of the Millennium, and the internet on Skye was painfully slow. We didn't have broadband. Sites like Google were barely in existence. Often I had to rely on copies of *Mountain Biking UK* for intel on what the likes of Martyn Ashton, Hans Rey, Martin Hawyes and Steve Peat had been up to. As I flicked through the features and read interview after interview, their characters seemed to bunny-hop off the page. Every story and adventure sounded mad, and their attitudes and experiments became an inspiration because they were working on a street style I could relate to (well, maybe not Peaty, but he's still a legend).

Elsewhere, I was picking up plenty of new tricks from a couple of *Mountain Biking UK* videos that I'd been given as a kid. One was a film called *Dirty Tricks and Cunning Stunts*. I used it as a personal style manual and 'how to' guide; the tape was soon worn thin. There was a funny story running throughout – the film was sold as being 'Fanciful. Instructional. Comical'. In the opening clip Martyn Ashton and Martin Hawyes had dressed up in wigs as part of a high-speed seventies-style police chase scene through London with a bunch of ninjas for good measure. Their effortless gapping was inspirational to Donnie, Jamie, Alex and me. We started trying back-hops, front-hops and gaps.

There were other influential riders along the way. The older I got, the more my collection of videos grew. The Americans Ryan Leech and Jeff Lenosky made a film called *Revolution* and I watched it pretty much every day. Seeing their work changed my perspective because *Revolution* had a little more street trials about it. Ryan and Jeff would carve about San Francisco and New York, gapping to railings and rolling G-turns and manuals. The speed of my riding picked up. We would watch *Revolution* over and over, as well as Jeff and Ryan's other films, like *Evolution* and *Contact*, round at Donnie's house while we were waiting for the liquid bitumen to dry on our brakes (the only way to make your brakes work for trials – it makes the rim surface stickier).

I was soon to get a shot at emulating my heroes as, that year, a trials competition was organized. It was taking place in Broadford, right next to where Donnie lived. I was buzzing. Graham Finney had arranged the event. He was a Skye man, and a major player in the healthy motorcycle trials scene on the island. The Skye Trials Club had been riding around the hills for quite a while, and Graham was used to setting up courses over rocks and through rivers, often in the pouring rain. This time, the club wanted to create a mountain-bike version in a less watery setting, and Graham was certainly enthusiastic about the idea. For a while he was keen on giving pushbike riders the same buzz of competition as experienced by the club's more long-standing members.

Motorbike trials were doing well on Skye, and a lot of comps took place every year, so it seemed only natural that a pedal version should also capture the imagination, especially given the relationship between both sports. Mountain-bike trials had originally started when the dad of Spanish motorcycle rider Ot Pi wanted him to master the style on a pedal version first. That created a cultural link between the two forms. And the course Graham laid out for us probably wasn't too dissimilar from the ones used for motorbikes. He had convinced the owner of a disused petrol station to let us borrow his land. The site was ringed with cars; some of them appeared to have been rusting since the 1930s. A circuit of wooden pallets was dotted around a bottle bank. The set-up might have been modest, but it still seemed pretty testing, and all the kids lining up with their bikes were incredibly excited.

The thing I noticed about Graham – apart from the fact

he seemed to be smiling permanently – was his accent. He talked fast and was the first bloke I'd ever met who used the term 'ken', as in, 'Do you ken Donnie?' (Do you know Donnie?) Or, 'It's pishing down, ken?' (It's raining quite heavily, know what I mean?) For a while, I kept wondering if Ken was a bloke who worked with the club. But Graham knew what he was doing, in spite of his unusual style of chat.

When the competition came around, the crowds were small – only around three or four people showed up to watch – but the event was great fun. I rode well, winning the events I was involved in. I even managed to finish two of the heats without dabbing, despite the fact that competition trials wasn't a style of riding I'd been used to. Graham was stoked, too. The following year he announced another event, but this time the catchment area was extended to competitors beyond the island. Before we knew it, several older lads from Inverness had signed up, and that was a big deal. Inverness riders – boys from the mainland – were mythical figures to us. The scene on Skye was non-existent compared to what we thought was going on across the water, and we'd all heard the rumours – *the legends* – of riders from Inverness. According to lads at school, they were able to pull off 360 jumps, no problem. Ten-foot drops were executed to perfection. Whenever I'd travelled to Inverness with Mum, I'd often see a rider manualling down the street. Before I'd had a chance to clock the make of his frame, he'd be around the corner and out of view in a flash. Sights like that only added to their prestigious status.

I suddenly felt intimidated. Trials events were a new thing for me, as was competition, and now the big boys were getting involved. It played on my mind. Shortly after signing up, I remember going to Donnie's house for tea. He could sense I was a little edgy.

'What's the matter?' he asked.

'I can't believe we'll have to compete against these guys, Donnie,' I admitted fearfully. 'We've been riding in our own little bubble on Skye. I haven't even met a rider outside of Portree High School, let alone ridden against one . . .'

I was right to be fearful. Those Inverness kids, when I saw them, had all the gear. There was a Monty, a Megamo, one or two Pashleys and an ultra-rare Brisa – it was clear to us that they meant business. Meanwhile, the circuit at Broadford had been upgraded. The pallets were back, but there were now several intimidating granite blocks, stacked in place using a JCB that Graham had borrowed from somewhere. He had also laid out a series of huge cable reels (the type the local council use to wind electric cables around), some old park benches – anything that might add a little extra difficulty to the circuit.

The promise of some serious competition had gathered a nice crowd, though most of the folk there were parents of the kids involved. Nevertheless, the extra pressure didn't affect me and I won three out of three trials, even though I was one of the youngest riders on show. But because I lacked a competitive edge the results weren't an issue for me. I wasn't spurred on to take competitions any more seriously

because I had come first again, but I could sense the importance of the event. That bubble, the one we'd been operating
in as we rode around Dunvegan, or at Broadford, had been
popped. The riders of the Highlands had joined together for
the first time. I made a lot of friends that day, which was
pretty important, given there hadn't been social media to
bring us together; Facebook and Twitter hadn't yet caught
fire. Even MySpace wasn't a thing. By actually meeting riders from outside of Skye, face to face – old school – I felt
looped into a bigger world.

All of a sudden, Dunvegan seemed even smaller. From
meeting the Inverness kids at Graham's champs, I knew
there was a whole world of riding out there, and I wanted to
be part of it. Also, there wasn't much going on in the way of
vocational options for me on Skye. I had to consider what
would happen once I'd left school. At one stage, Dad had all
these mad plans for me to go into the army, but I wasn't into
that at all. In 2002, I left Portree High with a few grades,
having just turned seventeen, determined to follow up my
dream of becoming a cycle mechanic. That's when I called
Bothy Bikes, a cycle store in Aviemore, the busy holiday
town set within the Cairngorms National Park. It was the
first speculative enquiry I'd ever made about a job.

I'd been dialled in to Aviemore by my Aunt Jean. She ran
a bunkhouse called the Glen Feshie Hostel for people travelling through the park, and her rooms were always booked.
The snow-capped Cairngorms mountain range stretched

into the distance, and there were plenty of beautiful trails criss-crossing the park, which had become popular with both mountain bikers and walkers. From the age of eight, I often stayed at Aviemore for family holidays, at Christmas and during the summer. I loved it. I could ride the trails whenever I wanted, and I always made sure to stop off at Bothy Bikes, so I could gawp at the stock.

Set on the high street, between a bunch of stores selling hiking gear, it was a goldmine for kids like me. Every time I walked in, the place felt like home. The shop floor was cluttered with iconic parts that I recognized from *Mountain Biking UK*, and I loved the whiff of it: Bothy Bikes smelled of inner tubes, tyres and chain-cleaner oil. There were suspension forks on the forecourt, wheels cluttering up the shop floor and cycles hanging from the ceiling. Aged twelve or thirteen, I'd stand in awe, staring at the full-suspension bikes, like the latest Pashley. I saw a Kona Stab Deluxe Downhill there for the first time, as well as a legendary Santa Cruz Super 8. All of the frames for sale were very expensive. Some of them cost in excess of a grand. They were unobtainable, but I didn't care. If I could have chosen a dream location to start my life as a cycle mechanic, it would have been there.

When I enquired about work, I was told by the shop owner, David Keegan, that they weren't in any need of a new mechanic, which was a kick in the teeth. But encouraged by the realization that I was at least trying to find myself a trade, Mum enrolled me on a City & Guilds course in Bike Mechanics down in Spalding, Lincolnshire. It meant a move away from home for a short period, but I loved it, and in class I studied loads of old techniques, like how to service Sturmey-Archer hubs, and cup and cone bottom-brackets. I even learned the techniques required for building my own wheels and, when a position eventually opened up in Bothy Bikes, shortly after the course had finished in 2003, I landed my dream job.

I was stoked. Getting a job in Bothy was a big deal, and that wasn't the only attraction in Aviemore. The place was a trials rider's paradise. As well as the trails cutting through the area, a car park in the middle of town was full of big boulders and stone from the local mountains. Nicknamed the Rocky Car Park, it was a fertile spot for any rider: there were random bollards to tyre-tap, benches and slanted signs to gap between, and railings to ride. Once work had finished I could jump from boulder to boulder under the floodlights. In that little square alone there were four times as many obstacles to be tried out than in the whole of Dunvegan. I'd upgraded my riding big time.

Scene Five

(<u>INT.</u>) Danny's childhood bedroom, Dunvegan

Danny and his bike have been shrunk, reduced to the size of a child's toy. The camera zooms in so we can see his helmet, gloves and pedals. He stares into the camera, nods, smiles and rides solo around a playground of oversized colouring pencils, playing cards and building blocks emblazoned with letters. They have been arranged to spell out 'DANNY'.

This is the trials course inside Danny's mind; he's using the obstacles he fantasized about riding as a kid — giant-sized board games, plastic tanks and models of Formula 1 racing cars. We even see him racing down a giant copy of the Dandy annual and carving around a Hot Wheels-style loop-the-loop . . .

Imaginate, 2013

Flair TyreTap to gap

5. The Rider's Eye

I like riding alone. I always have done, and probably always
will. It's a headspace thing. Because my friends lived several
miles away from Dunvegan, I learnt to make my own fun,
so it wasn't hard to get excited about gapping the flowerbed
containers in the Gun Shop. These days, it's the same: I usually ride solo, especially after a day spent working on shows,
planning videos and taking meetings. For a few hours I'll
cut about near my flat in Glasgow's city centre; if I'm back
home in Dunvegan, I'll run through familiar lines around
the village. And it's like any sport: I can have good days and
bad. On the off nights, I crash a lot. My head isn't into it and
the riding doesn't seem quite right. But when I'm locked in,
I feel strong, like I could tear the handlebars from my frame
with every trick. If I need to bunny-hop a four-feet-high
wall, I know I can go at it. My body and my bike will get
me there.

Before you start worrying about my social skills, I've got
plenty of mates, honest. I live in a big flat with seven friends.
A lot of them are involved with riding and have been hugely

influential in pretty much everything I've achieved so far. Like John Bailey: he runs a company called Vision Ramps alongside another friend, George Eccleston, and together they have constructed some of my set-ups in videos such as *Cascadia* and *Imaginate*. Two of the other guys, Ali C. and Duncan Shaw, are world-class trials riders, and Duncan currently manages a show I perform in called The Drop and Roll Tour. As you can imagine, our place looks like a cycle shop; there are wheels and parts everywhere. And whenever any of us goes out riding, it's usually alone.

Nobody minds; it's the done thing. Often, we'll pass each other in the dark, out on the streets with our headphones on. I reckon I've done 99 per cent of my life's cycling on my lonesome, and I guess the reason I love going out by myself is because I can ride what I want, when I want, and spend as much time on a particular line as I like, without having to worry about anyone else. I don't have to work from spots that I'm not into, and if ever I get bored of a space or an obstacle, I can move on to the next location.

When I'm riding, I'm always using my brain to take me somewhere new, and my visualizations can be so strong that, even when I'm at home and *thinking* about being on the bike, I'm imagining new tricks and fantasizing about new places to ride. I don't see street furniture like normal people do. I don't see everyday objects like normal people do. Instead, I look at the landscape through what I call the Rider's Eye: a filter that turns everything into an obstacle. In my mind, everything's a hurdle to jump over, an edge to gap to; *a challenge.* My subconscious is calculating all the spaces around me – that balcony ledge, those railings in the car park . . .

They don't even have to be real surfaces. When I was a kid, sitting at the dinner table, I'd use my fork as an imaginary bike. I'd imagine what it would be like to ride the curves of a super-sized spoon, or gap from the salt cellar to the pepper grinder and down on to my plate.

That later became the idea behind the 2013 film *Imaginate*. The seed was planted when I decided to come up with a grand concept – anything; scale no object – to do something in the Glasgow Transport Museum building, which had been lying empty for a little while. When we arrived there for the first time, I noticed that the owners had abandoned a lifesize train station from an old exhibition, and that's when my ideas started taking shape. I had a theme! The idea of returning to those childhood memories and upsizing my Dunvegan bedroom – a colourful, overblown playground of toys – into a giant obstacle course meant I was soon drawing up plans to make the most of the station's tracks and replica commuter platform. To add to the set-up, we later brought together huge building blocks and six-foot-tall plastic soldiers (mates dressed up in battle fatigues and covered in green paint). We even hired a decommissioned army tank and borrowed a Formula 1 car from Red Bull. The props were real, but the idea had come from my Rider's Eye.

Riding is only half of what I do. Creativity is the other side of my life, and I rarely quit daydreaming. I often have to force myself to stop thinking about the bike when I go to bed. I struggle to fall asleep otherwise. It's the same when I'm awake. Whenever I go somewhere new, the first thing I think is, What can I jump off in this place? The Rider's Eye begins working, assessing size, space and the distances required to gap between different objects. Straightaway, I wonder if there's an obstacle or shape that could be used for a new video. I can drift off for ages, lost in my own head-space. I might be somewhere like a shopping centre, mooching about a clothes store, but I'm actually seeing beyond the shop windows and the mannequins in the fore-ground and focusing on the escalators behind instead.

Hmm, I'll think. I could bump off that recycling bin out-side and hop up on to that moving rail . . .

The visualizations are so vivid that I can even feel the sensation of my landing after a jump, and the crunch of tyres, the bite of the brakes. It happens subconsciously and I'm forever doing it, even in the car. I can lose twenty min-utes daydreaming about an idea, which is a problem if ever I'm bombing down the motorway.

I think this vivid daydreaming has always come naturally to me. At school I focused on practical subjects like craft and design, physics and PE, but I struggled with anything to do with writing because I was dyslexic. Mum and Dad realized that something was up with me when I was small. Not when I was throwing myself out of a tree or rag-dolling down hills, but because I seemed unable to concentrate in class. My attention span was terrible. A lot of schoolwork revolved around being able to read and write and, because I wasn't as good at it as some of the other children, I would mess about a bit. That was probably considered a problem for me as a kid, especially when it came to stuff like grades and exams.

This lack of concentration wasn't exactly a step towards trials biking – I'd imagine my schooling was no different to a lot of riders' – but some experts have tried to link my dyslexia to the creative ideas I've come up with. When I attended the annual Edinburgh Science Festival, I was interviewed onstage in a show called 'Tunnel Vision'. Hosted by Professor Ian Robertson, a psychologist and founding director of the Trinity College Institute of Neuroscience in Dublin, our chat dialled into what goes on in my brain whenever I'm on the bike, riding around alone in Glasgow, or thinking up video ideas.

'You find it hard to concentrate on a book,' he said. 'You're not good at reading, but it strikes me from watching *Imaginate* that you have a powerful visual imagination . . .'

I told him how I was never good at reading and writing in school, and I often became unfocused in class. I then explained how I wasn't good at art either (in a traditional drawing sense), but that I found physical or image-based activities easier.

Professor Robertson asked if I ever drew sketches during video-planning sessions. I explained that I did, though they were hardly masterpieces. Whenever I come up with new ideas I draw wee stick men on two wheels. They're rough sketches, 'a drawing of whatever action or obstacle I'm going to attempt,' I said. 'I save them all in a big list. I have books at home full of random tricks and, if a new project comes up, I'll look through them to remind me of stuff. There are so many possibilities on the bike, they're endless, so it's nice to have certain things in the back of my mind . . .'

My notepads aren't the only thing overflowing with ideas. I've crammed an iPhone with pages and pages of brainstorm sessions. Sometimes I can come up with several ideas a day, such as:

— Russian Final Frontier
— Becoming the Invisible Man (with the Queen song)???
— The Fridge (spoof film of my viral video, *The Ridge*?)
— *Bugsy Malone*: I ride around in a scene similar to the 'We could have been anything that we wanted to be' part from the kids' musical
— Straight Outta Scotland/Compton edit – a play on the NWA movie

Professor Robertson suggested that dyslexia might have come into play with regards to my creativity. His theory was that people use the brain in one of two different ways. The first revolves around analytical, logical and verbal thinking – the stuff that's taught by schools during English and history lessons. The other form is mainly image-based thinking – used in the creative or practical subjects, such as art or woodwork, where people need to see images rather than words in their head to be successful.

'The thing is, those two halves are in competition with each other,' he said. 'They inhibit each other. Children of three or four think largely in images, but most of them lose that capacity because the verbal analytics system of school is built up so strongly that it inhibits the other one. Danny, it strikes me that, had you not been a bit weak on the verbal side of things, you might not have developed the rich visual world that underpins you as a creative producer, not just a stunt cyclist. Does that make sense?'

I nodded, but I wasn't sure. It was a fascinating theory, but I don't think I'm that different to any other rider. I have a strong imagination that I've fortunately been able to turn into a series of videos and interesting tricks. My Rider's Eye has kept me constantly occupied. Fingers crossed it keeps working for a while yet.

Scene Six

<u>FADE IN</u>

(<u>EXT.</u>) A supermarket car park, Aviemore

A grainy black-and-white shot of young Danny.
He is eighteen years old, skinny. Riding his
twenty-six-inch Titanium trials bike, he
approaches a bin, hopping up to the top on his
back wheel. He adjusts his position slightly
before dropping off, first on to a stone wall and
then several feet below to another wall which
slopes away. He later gaps two rocks over a
stream and tyre taps on a tree from a grass
bank. This is our first glimpse of Danny, the
YouTube trials rider.

                                    TartyBikes, 2006

AVIMORE EDIT

up to Rails to G Ewn

police

Tire tap tree

Blunt to Backwards Manual

360 Nose Pick on Back of Bench

6. An Accidental Viral

Bikes came and went, but I've always hung on to the frames, no matter how smashed up they were. More or less every chapter in my trial-biking life has been kept in a collection, including a series of Pashleys that were worn out, even before I'd got to Aviemore. Sadly, my Kona from Dunvegan had been wrecked by the time I'd turned thirteen (the head tube is the only part I have left), but the others are all there. Some of the parts are stashed away in my Glasgow flat; others have been stored at my mum and dad's house on Skye.

In my early teens, I obsessed over owning a Pace, as used by six-times British National Trials champion Chris Akrigg. It was a cool-looking bike, arriving with a box section made from milled-out aluminium tubes. At school I'd draw sketches of the Pace on the pages of my jotter, rather than focusing on physics. When I finally bought one from Bothy Bikes it was my most prized possession, but that wasn't going to stop me from riding it pretty hard. The frame was later snapped in two after only five months' riding, typically. It's back in my house in Dunvegan, hanging on the wall.

The Pace was a rare beast, and finding one required patience. The style that Chris had been riding at the time came in gunmetal silver, but the one I really wanted was fire-engine red. It looked amazing, but customers had to wait around eight months for it because the design was a limited edition. I decided to sit through the best part of a year to get one, relying on the charity of my mates to keep me riding. I'd borrow frames from the lads on Skye, which I'd proceed to smash up pretty badly, and by the time my brand-new Pace arrived I owed a ton of parts.

As my riding advanced, the bikes began to suffer, not that I'd feel too sorry about it. I've always viewed them as tools for the job, and 'mechanical sympathy' wasn't going to stand in the way of any progress. So I was willing to smash up my forks, and my wheels, especially when I was working on new stunts like tailwhips – a trick that involves me doing a bunny-hop and kicking the frame around the steering tube. While it was spinning 360 degrees, I would have to jump up before landing back on the pedals. It was quite a tricky manoeuvre, and every fourth or fifth attempt I would have to straighten my back wheel because it had buckled during the landing. My gaps and general riding were also becoming more ambitious. I was constantly trying to jump large distances between walls and boulders in the Rocky Car Park, and crashing all the time.

At night, I'd ride around for a few hours. Because so many people visiting the area were into hiking, skiing or mountain biking, I'd rarely get any hassle. The locals were nice folk, too. They would watch me in the town centre, jumping the rocks after dark, in the pouring rain with friends, or out by myself in the ice and snow. Nobody was bothered, not like they had been in Dunvegan. To them I was just another part of Aviemore's furniture.

I was becoming interested in the bigger scene more and more. Chris Akrigg was a rider who was influencing me, and I pored over his articles in *Mountain Biking UK*. I loved reading about him because his style was so fresh; he was aggressive. Chris would ride his Pace like a motorcycle, especially during comps. Most riders hop their bike between obstacles when working through sections, for accuracy. Not Chris. He would move fast but fluidly, smashing his way through a course without stopping. Chris was constantly moving and gapping, but Martyn Ashton was different. He would hop through sections on his back wheel with ease. He had a precise technique, and there were more tricks in his videos, what with his 180 gaps and 360 drops. While in Aviemore, I'd often try to dial in to Chris's or Martyn's style. When it came to finessing a stunt of my own, I would say, 'Right, I'm gonna do this one like Martyn!' It was a way of pushing myself.

Meanwhile, several exciting styles had broken out in trials, which were proving to be equally inspirational. A movement called TGS (Taps, Gaps and Sidehops) came through where riders like Neil Tunnicliffe and Craig Lee Scott were gapping and hopping incredible distances. TGS had emerged from mountain biking, and it blew my mind. I didn't have a laptop and Aunt Jean didn't have a computer, so I was a little disconnected from what was going on. But when I finally got to see them, I was astounded. They were jumping a foot higher than anyone had ever done before, and gapping from walls on to roadside railings while landing front wheel first. Neil and Craig had upped the game, and I felt a little disheartened. While Martyn and Chris's riding had felt achievable, those guys had raised the bar much higher. Still, it didn't stop me from trying to emulate them, not that I was too successful.

When it came to work, Bothy Bikes paid me like an apprentice, but the low wages didn't matter because I was living in Aunt Jean's bunkhouse and eating like a king: on the menu were plates of salmon, steak and Dauphinoise potatoes and big seafood lasagnes. Her food was legendary. Luckily, Aunt Jean's calorific dinners were burnt off every day during an eleven-mile ride to work on an old road cycle, and once I'd arrived at the store I'd make the most of all the perks that came with being at a cool outpost like Bothy. I got to work on high-end bikes while chatting – maybe slightly geekily – to the customers about their riding. Sometimes, I was able to pick up parts and frames at trade prices, and it soon dawned on me that I was on to a winner: without that discount I would have had to earn a lot more money elsewhere to afford the stuff I was picking up at the shop.

It was a nice place to work, too. Bothy Bikes had moved from Aviemore High Street and was now situated in the middle of the national park, where it catered for everyone, from kids to expert riders. For the most part, it specialized in top-of-the-range mountain bikes like Santa Cruz, Scott and Kona, though a lot of trade was also focused on hiring out cycles to tourists who wanted to explore the trails. If you were into your riding, it was a cool place to explore. The new store resembled an old bothy, which, in Scotland, is a basic hut used for shelter or storage in the mountains; they were often left unlocked for anyone to use, free. The shop was back from the road, nestling in the woods like a house from some old fairy-tale. Whenever it snowed, which it did a lot in the winter, there was a real picture-postcard vibe.

There was nowhere else I'd rather have been working than Bothy, because I could ride as much as possible (when I wasn't working in the store and listening to DJ Shadow or Rage Against The Machine, that is) and my day usually started with that ride to work. I'd often be the first lad to arrive. Once it got to lunch, I'd ride for another fifty-five minutes on my trials bike, wolfing down a sandwich and a packet of fig rolls during the last few minutes, before setting off back. There was a big hill called Craigellachie that loomed over the shop. If I was quick I could push all the way to the top and burn down, hitting a great trail on the descent, often on a demo mountain bike I'd borrowed from Bothy. A lot of the time I'd ride with Mark, who also worked in the shop. At clocking-off time, I'd hit the Rocky Car Park for a few hours on my trials bike, later stashing it away before travelling those eleven miles home on the road cycle. I must have been exceptionally fit.

I wasn't thinking, Oh, one day I want to be a professional rider. The idea had never crossed my mind. Whenever friends suggested I should write a letter to manufacturers, asking for sponsorship and free equipment, I shrugged it off. It was the done thing in mountain biking, especially if a rider had a profile of sorts. But I always cringed whenever the idea came up in conversation; I felt embarrassed at the thought of asking for hand-outs, and I didn't think it would come to anything. Besides, I'd seen people try it in Bothy: young riders bigging themselves up over the phone in a desperate attempt to blag free gear. Their argument was that they could advertise our store by racing with a bike, or jacket, branded with the shop logo. I wasn't into that. I'd always believed that if you were good enough at something then the right people would eventually take notice. Besides, I was already living the dream, and at trade prices, too.

In 2005, internet-based viral videos were in their infancy. MySpace was barely up and running; the idea of unsigned bands scoring a record deal from homespun recordings they'd placed online, like Lily Allen or Arctic Monkeys, was still pretty unusual. None of the top riders in mountain biking or BMX had caught on to the importance of social media either, and sites like YouTube or Twitter just didn't have the power they enjoy now. The internet, to us, was untapped.

When a mate of mine, Nash Masson, suggested I make a video of stunts around Aviemore, I didn't think anything of it. I thought it might be a bit of a laugh. I had made a few videos with Donnie and Jamie, but the idea of it going beyond our circle of mates had never struck me. Still, I was into it, and I went into Inverness and bought a £300 camera, before convincing Nash to do all the filming. I'm not sure if he had even done videos before, but he seemed keen.

For a day, we documented the riding I had been doing around Aviemore. I hopped on to some silver rails in front of the local supermarket, before capturing a few flowing lines in the Rocky Car Park. There was a pub nearby called Mambo's. It had an interesting slope that led up to a bin. I could tap a tyre on the top and then gap back, landing the rear wheel into a backwards manual (without putting the front down). It was a wheelie in reverse, but a fair bit trickier. I gapped about on rocks and jumped over a little river that ran through the town.

Earlier in the year, Nash and I had broken into Santa Claus Land, a derelict theme park in Aviemore, and raided the soft play area for foam. The site was set for demolition so we snuck in one day and tore bags of the stuff from the walls. Our plan had been to pile it up in front of a dirt ramp, which we'd built nearby, and, with our makeshift foam pit, we'd try flips for the first time. Whenever we went to the jump, we would throw ourselves off the ramp and land in the padding that had been strategically placed to soften the fall. My first back-flip attempts were a disaster. The foam would gobble up the wheels as I landed, which could cause some uncomfortable landings – upon impact, various body parts squished against the frame.

I quickly moved on to front flips, which was a milestone. Unless a rider had a skatepark with a foam pit nearby, it was difficult for them to find anywhere safe to learn that style of jumping. Luckily, our DIY ramp was just the place and, to my surprise, after one or two attempts, I found I could bring the bike around quite easily. It was the first time I'd been upside down on two wheels, and it was fun. I didn't land any to dirt, but it gave me a feel for the technique that was needed to perform a flip. For our home-made film we recorded a series of attempts and saved the best ones on the camera.

The idea of uploading the clips to MySpace or YouTube, the most popular social media at that time, hadn't crossed my mind. Nash's clips were purely for personal use, a bunch of random tricks in no particular order to watch with mates. I think the film sat on my camcorder at home for a year before Donnie picked up on it when I'd returned home to Skye at Christmas in 2006.

He took one look at the stunts and my crash into the Santa Claus Land mats and seemed impressed.

'Give me the video, Daniel, I'll upload it,' he said.

'What do you mean?' I asked. I wasn't entirely sure what he was going on about. When it came to the internet, I wasn't clued up at all.

'Just give us the tapes,' he said. 'My brother, Gordon, will edit the stunts together and we'll put it online. We'll piece together a little clip and put it on YouTube.'

I agreed and we named our film *TartyBikes* after an internet store that had given me a few discounted parts. It wasn't long before Gordon had announced that my film was uploaded. I checked it out once but, after a few weeks, I'd completely forgotten about it. The next time I got on to a computer, 250,000 views had been clocked up. The video was also going down well on a riding site called Trials Forum, not that I could keep up. Because I didn't have a laptop or computer at home, I'd check out the viewing figures at a friend's house. Whenever I logged on, I'd be shocked by the results, especially once I realized that a million people had seen it on YouTube. At first, I thought it was funny. It had seemed like a bit of a laugh, nothing more. I never believed anything would come of my making a riding video in a car park with a modest camera.

If only I had known.

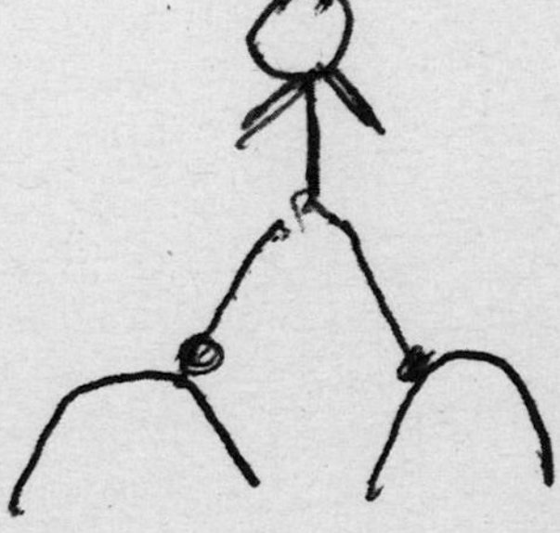

Scene Seven

<u>FADE IN</u>

(<u>EXT.</u>) A trials course, Aberfeldy

A grey, rainy day. Danny's friend Duncan Shaw
is on his bike atop a small steel rig, no more
than five feet in height. Below him on the grass,
Danny lays flat on his back. He looks nervous.
His hands are positioned protectively over
his crotch.

Duncan rides to the edge and looks down. He hops
on to his back wheel and drops off the rig. The
tyre lands between Danny's legs, perilously
close to crushing his nether regions, which have
since been covered with a helmet. Duncan rides
away. A concerned audience looks on — and
winces.

Danny MacAskill and the
Clan in Aberfeldy, 2009

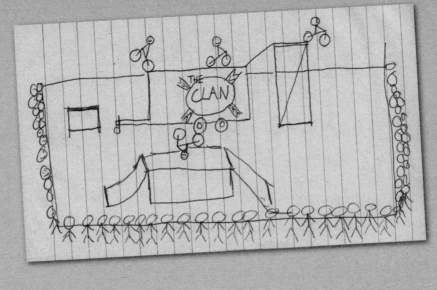

7. The Clan

By summer 2006 I'd ridden Aviemore to death. I had tried every line in town for three years, smashing through the Rocky Car Park, while working on new tricks. But I had an itchy feeling, the urge to move on, and it was a mood I could put down to a chance encounter with Fraser McNeil, one of the best trials cyclists in Edinburgh. We had bumped into each other in Bothy Bikes and got talking.

'Head to Edinburgh for a bit,' he said. 'Come and check the place out. There's tons of great walls, rails and other stuff in town. We're making some films, too. You should get involved . . .'

I travelled to the city by train a couple of times, just to get a sense of the place, and I picked up a good feeling. Even though I'd grown up in the Highlands, Edinburgh still felt more like a big town than a city, and I reckoned it might be the perfect home, both to improve my riding and to get me close to a different scene. I needed new horizons, and Scotland's capital was just the place. Meanwhile, some friends from Bothy Bikes had moved into the city, taking up jobs in a shop called Macdonald Cycles. Once they'd got wind that I was moving over, they talked their manager into taking me on as a mechanic. It proved to be a lucky break.

Summer had kicked in, the weather was roasting hot, and there were endless places to ride on my doorstep. Everything felt fresh and exciting. In terms of street trials, I was doing the same stuff that I was doing in Aviemore, but in Edinburgh there were some legendary spots, such as Bristo Square, which had stair sets and was the unofficial hub for riders. Most days, twenty or thirty skateboarders would gather there, as well as a few BMXers. I would ride at the National Gallery, over a sculpture that I later nicknamed 'The Cake'. The Scottish Parliament had some huge concrete blocks, which were good for jumping over. All featured in my 2009 film, *Inspired Bicycles*.

There was plenty of mountain biking to do, which was a bonus, such as on Arthur's Seat, the four-hundred-foot-high hill in the middle of town. On a warm evening I would head for the top, making a couple of illegal runs up and down the paths (cycling on Arthur's Seat had been banned). I would also cycle from home into the Pentland Hills for my fix of trails, or travel south of Edinburgh for an hour or so to Glentress Forest, a Mecca for mountain bikers. The possibilities seemed endless.

It wasn't all plain sailing, though. I snapped plenty of bikes that first year, mainly because I'd learned a riding technique called a hook, a manoeuvre that involved throwing myself at a wall and bouncing on to the top. The basic technique was this: I would ride towards a wall of around six feet in height and, with about eight feet of tarmac to go, I'd pull up, lifting my front wheel just over the top edge as I hit the wall – that was the 'hook'. My back wheel would then bump into the brick face; momentum flexed the fork, allowing me to air up on to the top, landing on my back wheel.

In Aviemore I could manage hooks of around four feet. But in Edinburgh, where I had new stair sets, walls and railings to jump on, my riding was coming on in leaps and bounds, although I kept wrecking the bikes and my body in the process. I'd crack a bike frame every couple of weeks, and I picked up an assortment of injuries: a broken wrist, a dislocated index finger, torn ligaments in my right and left ankles and innumerable bruises to my heels (before I got a pair of decent shoes). But like Bothy, Macdonald Cycles carried a pretty laid-back management style, and nobody seemed to mind the slings and casts I had to wear sometimes, even though it was a busy store. The shop had been on Morrison Street for years and, while it catered for the mountain-bike crowd in part, it was mainly tailored towards the commuter cyclist. It was *the* cycle shop in town during the eighties when racers by the likes of Raleigh were hugely popular.

Most of the time, I was stationed in the Cave – the basement. From there, I spent my days repairing shonky bikes, undisturbed by a rush of customers asking for helmets or puncture-repair kits up on the shop floor. The Cave was a cool spot; it had character – an underground labyrinth of parts, old, cool frames and boxes and boxes of stock. My music, Judas Priest included, would blare out of the stereo. Parts and tools never complained or talked back, and there wasn't a single day when I dreaded going into the Cave.

Clocking off was fun because once the shop had closed, there was usually a street race home. I rode about town on a little Kona that I'd nicknamed 'The Wee Commuty', and as soon as six o'clock came around, a charge back to the flat would begin. My mates George and John would start along-side me – the guys that would later go on to found Vision Ramps – and it was wild. We'd draught the buses along Princes Street and sprint downhill along Lothian Road and Leith Walk. There was a big roundabout near our place, and the three of us would often straight-line it across, slicing up the streets before skidding into the front porch, knackered. There were a few tumbles along the way, but it didn't matter. If ever I showed up to work with my fingers strapped up, unable to tinker with the repairs, Colin would send me to work on the shop floor. It wasn't the Cave, but I enjoyed it, even if the cus-tomers did pester me for puncture kits and answer back.

I was lucky. With all the smashes and scrapes, I could buy brand-new replacement parts from the store at low cost. I'd also picked up some modest sponsorship deals from a couple of compan-ies while working in Bothy. (Not that I'd asked for them.) The first was with TartyBikes, a trials company I'd come across while I was riding down south one weekend, and, as I men-tioned, the titular inspiration for my first film. I was told I could call them if I needed new parts. Whenever I did, a box would arrive shortly afterwards. Meanwhile, one of the guys who ran TartyBikes, Dave Cleaver, had designs to start a new bike brand of his own. One afternoon, I was wandering around a trade show at the Conference Centre in Birmingham when he pulled me to one side.

'I want you to ride for Inspired Bicycles, my new company,' said Dave. 'Fancy it?'

I was going through parts like nobody's business, so I considered the offer an amazing opportunity, because Dave reckoned he could supply me with plenty of free equipment. Once I'd signed with Inspired Bicycles, I was told I'd be using their new prototype frames and forks, the earliest of which was a twenty-four-inch street-trials bike – the first I'd ever ridden of that size and one of the first that was focused on my style of tricks. Street-trials manufacturers were quite unusual, probably because the scene was so small. There were Inspired and a couple of other brands, but that was it.

The Inspired was all about manoeuvrability. It came with a set of super-powerful brakes, and I could have complete control over my movement. It had short chainstays on the rear, so the frame sat comfortably on the back wheel whenever I was manualling. Also, because the wheels were smaller, and didn't bend all the time like they did with a regular trials bike, tricks like tailwhips, 360s and hooks felt easier. When I rode the Inspired for the first time, it felt like the bike I'd always been looking for.

The other key component was the saddle. Unlike some other trials bikes, the Inspired had a seat (which trials riders rarely use), and that would soon prove to be an important feature. When I later made films like *Inspired Bicycles*, people accepted my riding, even though it was very specialized. Dave's design appeared to the wider world like a conventional cycle – a BMXer or a road cyclist could look at the frame and relate to it – whereas other trial-bike designs were more niche. The Inspired was recognizable, *familiar*. It didn't look as if I was riding about on a pogo stick.

I'm not that tall – around five foot eight – and the smaller-sized wheels meant I could bunny-hop with ease. Once I began using the Inspired around town, the technical differences had a massive impact on my riding. And every time I snapped a part – my head tube, the fork – I would call Dave, informing him how I'd wrecked his latest prototype. He'd listen to my thoughts and tailor the replacement parts accordingly. Together, we were developing a bike that I could grow with. It was the beginning of a strong partnership.

Having settled into Edinburgh life, I was soon mixing with a bunch of influential riders from all over the place. Although there weren't many trials riders, there was a healthy two-wheeled scene in the city, and lots of them would visit the shop for parts and repairs. It didn't matter if you rode downhill, BMX, road bikes or trials – we loved riding, there was no cliqueness and, at the end of the day, we shared a passion for bikes.

Being surrounded by that creativity soon rubbed off on me, and it wasn't long before I'd dreamt up a plan of my own: a touring trials show called 'the Clan'. My partner-in-crime for this project was Iain Withers, a former courier and cycling entrepreneur. Iain had established a company called MB7 which specialized in skills courses and guided trails riding around the area. Meanwhile, I had been doing some work with the Forestry Commission, not chopping down trees but riding with their stunt demo team, the 7Stanes Cycle Display Team. We performed at mountain-bike centres in the Borders. They had a purpose-built trials rig, with a few boxes and some rails to jump over. The work proved to be a nice little earner alongside my job in Macdonald Cycles, but I knew I could do something of my own. In 2008, when Iain and I got together during a show in Birmingham, we discussed starting a new team.

In terms of the spectator aspect of trials, I had a taste of competitions way back when, but it never really rang true with me. I was just more suited to the street style of riding. Out on the street, I can try a trick fifty times out in the rain, wind or, when I'm lucky, sun before getting close to mastering it. Competitions weren't like that. They were more restrictive and had more barriers. I would rather have no rules, stick my head-phones in and just roam the streets in my bubble, looking for the next ledge to hop, the next phone box to bump on to and the next wall to manual. The competition scene wasn't for me . . .

Shows were different. They were a non-competitive for-mat where riders performed on boxes, rails and ramps at agricultural shows, music festivals and corporate fun days. The biggest example of a successful set-up was the Animal Bike Tour. A show branded by the clothing company of the same name and headlined by Martyn Ashton, Animal was a hit. It wasn't uncommon to see them performing at heavy-weight events like the British MotoGP at Silverstone. Iain and myself weren't aiming that high – not yet – but we knew there were some interesting business opportunities to be generated if we were to start up in Scotland.

The pair of us quickly came up with the name the Clan, and began drawing together a line-up comprising the top guys in Scottish trials. Among them was Duncan Shaw, a UK champ, and my old mate Nash Masson. Fraser McNeil, who had been so influential in getting me to Edinburgh, joined soon after and, once word got around, offers flooded in. There were requests from agricultural shows, cycle events, races and exhibitions – all sorts. We made a portable street course of jump boxes, a bunny-hop bar and a ten-foot-tall tower. Before long, our schedules were so packed that it was impossible for me to head back to Skye at week-ends; in twelve months, we did thirty school shows, as well as thirty paid performances. I loved it. The crowds were great but, most importantly, I was touring with friends and making a living from my riding.

I even managed my first back flip that year, which was a rush. It happened in the opening Clan show of 2008 in the Loch Lomond Aquarium. We had built a brand-new jump box and in practice the day before I finally got my head around landing a back flip to hard ground, rather than in a foam pit. I'd learned that the technique (pedalling up to the ramp as fast as I could, pulling backwards, but not too hard, while looking up) worked quite easily. All I had to do was focus on the landing, and I was upside down for such a short period of time that it quickly came into view. I had broken a lot of parts during my practice sessions by landing just outside the pit – the impact bent forks, wheels and bars. Having back flips dialled was such a confidence booster that I decided to give it a go at Loch Lomond the next day. I had them on lock after that.

Meanwhile, at Macdonald Cycles, I was mixing with a ton of folk outside of trials – BMXers, mainly. That's around the time I met Dave Sowerby, one of the best in Scotland, and certainly one of the top film-makers on the scene. Every year he would make one or two amazing DVDs. When it came to BMX videos, Dave was formidable, and he made films with Proper Bike Co. and Nike, and would later build BSD into the brand it is today.

Dave was looking for a flatmate at his place in the Marchmont area of Edinburgh. I told him I was up for moving in, and I soon realized my new home was the local hub for BMXers. Whenever a new film came out, Dave would get a copy of the DVD and everybody would visit our place for the screening. Those were good times. Regularly, there would be twenty different folk sitting around, getting into the latest release (or an episode of *The Mighty Boosh*). As I watched, Dave would point out the technical details on each stunt. He'd talk about the stylistic points that made a shot work; we'd discuss the editing and even the soundtrack. These things hadn't been on my radar when I was riding around Dunvegan or Aviemore.

One evening in 2008, Dave changed the way I thought about riding – *for ever*. He had brought home a movie called *Grounded*, produced by the skate and BMX brand Etnies. The film featured Ruben Alcantara, a legendary BMXer; his inverts were always featured in BMX mags. Apparently, Ruben had set out to deliver his greatest ever film during the making of *Grounded*, and it showed. He did a series of ground-breaking (. . . probably why he called it *Grounded*) tricks that were coined 'Ruben Wallrides' because they blew everyone's minds – he was putting two wheels on vertical walls in places where nobody thought possible. *Grounded* was a game-changer.

Not long afterwards, Dave had a pretty serious crash and spiral-fractured his shinbone. While cutting about at Perth skatepark, he'd attempted a huge gap over a railing but came up short, clipping his back wheel on the edge. Dave had to jump clear as his bike clattered to the ground, but he fell pretty hard. He's a big guy, well over six feet tall and, as he landed, his shin snapped underneath him and shattered. For six weeks Dave was in a cast, unable to move around without crutches and inca-pable of riding or filming, which must have driven him mad.

One afternoon, while we were both hanging out in the flat, he offered to film some of my stunts and tricks. I knew what he was capable of creating. It felt like an honour – I wouldn't have dared ask him myself.

'Sure,' I told him. 'I'd love to.'

I mean, how often do you get to work with one of BMX's greatest film-makers?

Scene Eight

Princes Street Gardens, Edinburgh

The flowers of Princes Street Gardens are in the foreground. In the background, Danny sits on a wall that overlooks the gardens, his feet dangling over the edge. Beneath him is a fall of eighteen feet to a grass slope that runs down to a footpath.

<u>FADE OUT</u>

We cut to Danny, now on his bike, standing in the same spot. He edges forward, jumps off and spins, landing briefly on a thin ledge positioned at 90 degrees to him. His bike rebounds and he drops again, this time twisting another 90 degrees. Danny lands on the grass incline below and rides down to the path. As he rides off, several shocked onlookers crowd around the ledge and stare . . .

Inspired Bicycles, 2009

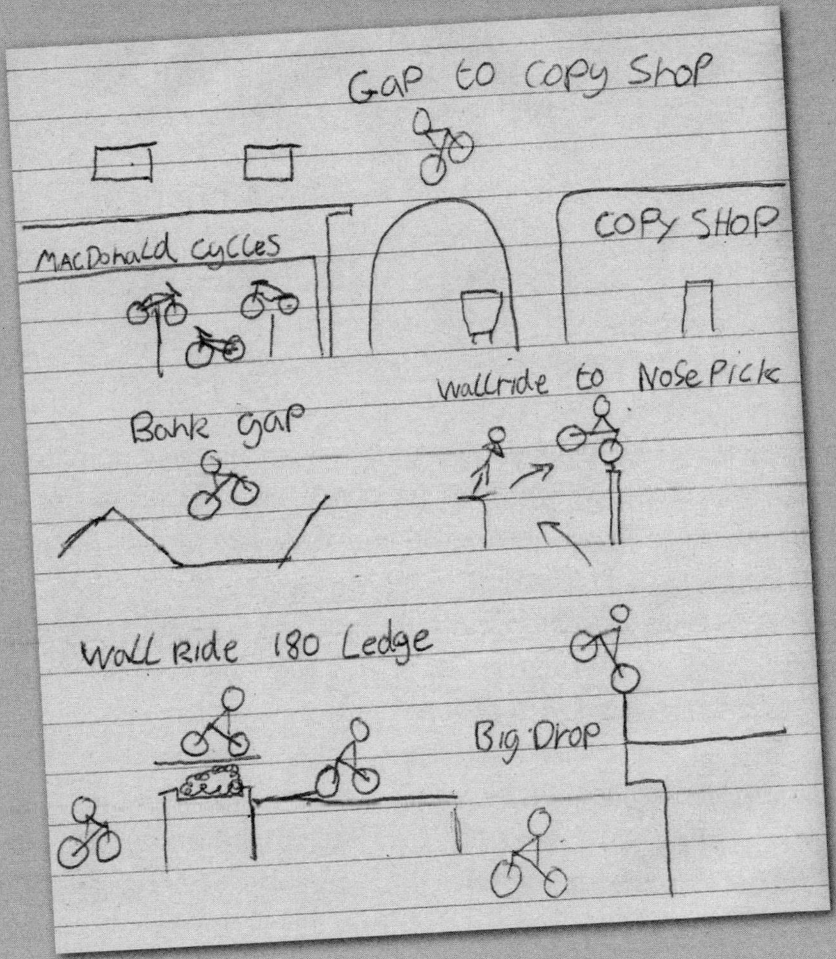

Gap to copy shop

MacDonald cycles

COPY SHOP

Bank gap

Wallride to Nose Pick

Wall Ride 180 Ledge

Big Drop

8. Riding the Roofs

We went up to the art college on the first filming session in October 2008. The idea was to scope out a few lines with potential, stuff that I had been looking at trying for a while. It was a crisp autumn day. There was a low sun, and Dave filmed everything through his fish-eye lens, which created a bowl effect on all the images. It was the first time I'd seen my riding captured in that style.

We got a few tricks down; the toughest shot of the lot was a bump 180 over a roadside rail. That took a while to land the way we wanted. In another scene I linked a wallride to a 180 over a flowerbed, which went into a six-foot drop below, and those clips became a solid foundation for our filming. From then on, I made mental notes on more spots around the city. I've got this amazing opportunity here, I kept thinking. What else can I do? My ideas grew bigger and bolder.

I became obsessed with every shot. The idea of putting together a film with Dave had encouraged me to set my sights high. Riding had just been about *riding* before; now I was picturing how things would look on camera, and I wanted to push myself in the same way as Ruben had during the making of *Grounded*. Since moving to Edinburgh, I'd been noticing new lines and walls on a daily basis, but some of them were too risky to attempt for fun. Now, with a camera capturing everything, those obstacles became more appealing; they were worth taking a shot at. One idea featured a wall overlooking Princes Street Gardens. It had an eighteen-foot drop on one side, which ran down to a steep grass bank, and it was full on, but I reckoned just within my capabilities. As soon as I saw it, I knew it was a line I'd have to go at, because it was on a scale I'd never attempted in the past. When the weather was too horrible for filming, I'd stop by there during my commute, braving the snow and ice to stand at the top and stare.

One day, I'm gonna do that, I'd think, looking down at the bank, my stomach tightening. Just assessing the wall, and its height, gave me the fear.

I soon built a sense of the quality control required to make a decent video. After each trick, I'd circle back to where Dave was shooting, his tall frame crouched over the camera so he could show me a replay or deliver directional cues. Spinning goofy was bad, so were bitch cranks out of a manual. Every trick had to look smooth, with as few correction hops as possible.

The pair of us got into a productive routine. I was working in Macdonald Cycles during the week and performing shows with the Clan as and when they came up at weekends. Luckily, the shop shifts were flexible and I could choose which days to take off, so I'd be forever checking the weather forecasts to catch the best days for riding. If I couldn't make time when the sun was shining, we would get together during the lunch break.

Dave was so patient with me. Initially, we reckoned on the project lasting no more than a few weeks. As autumn turned into winter and the conditions became tougher, *wetter*, we were forced into stepping back for a while. There were plenty of lines I'd wanted to attempt, but the surfaces had to be bone-dry, especially that eighteen-foot drop into Princes Street Gardens, which needed me to gap out towards a copper ledge before freefalling on to the bank below. Any moisture on top and the bike was going to slip off, taking me with it. And as for riding along a set of metal railings in the rain? Forget it. There was too much room for error.

Come November, we knew we'd have to bide our time for the perfect day, but I was optimistic. I'd look out of my window as soon as I woke up. If I saw a bright blue sky I'd knock on Dave's door to stir him. He'd often have to work late into the night on other projects, but most of the time he was up for filming. That was incredibly generous. There was zero budget for Dave's work; the only money we spent was on tape.

If the wet and the windy days had an upside, it was that I could find the time to scheme. One lunchtime, I wandered out of the Cave to buy a sandwich. Morrison Street was busy, and as I stood waiting for the traffic to pass I stared absent-mindedly at the shop fronts. The closest neighbour to us was CopyStop, a printing store, and an alley named Chuckie Pend divided our two doorways. Both shops had flat roofs above their entrances and I reckoned the space between them was around twelve feet.

What if I could jump that?

I stopped myself short. I figured something up there would probably stop me from taking a run-up, like a corrugated surface. But when I mentioned the idea to Nash, who was also working at Macdonald Cycles, he shook his head.

'Nah, I've been up there,' he said. 'It's completely flat.'

I couldn't wait to tell Dave.

I had no care at the time for whether or not this idea had scope, if it would branch out of my little bubble, out of trials, or even out of the mountain-bike scene. It really wasn't on my radar. However, Dave was encouraging. He wasn't one for dishing out praise, but I could tell that he was into the shooting as much as I was. With every week he added extra details, clips that would give the viewer a story, as well as some unusual angles to showcase the riding. There were views of Edinburgh's spires at sunset; he wanted to open the film with a silhouette of the city castle. While this was a street film in vibe, Dave also wanted to set a mood through the editing. He had grown up in and around the area. Showing off Edinburgh became important.

I focused on planning as many new lines as I could. Some of them were one-shot stunts; others included a sequence of tricks, like in a BMX or skate film. One of these took place outside the library at George Square. I 360'd down a five set of stairs, travelled along a hill below, bunny-hopped a bollard before turning sharply and hooking a five-and-a-half-foot wall; moving away from the camera, I carved back around, finishing the clip off with a 360 drop down a ten set.

There were a couple of bangers, too. I fought the fear and hit the huge slope at Princes Street Garden, though the stunt took me two days. Our first attempt happened under a crystal-clear sky, but it was blowing a hoolie and, as I left the flat, I noticed that the street sign was bending with the gust. This is not looking good, I thought, but nothing was going to tempt me into bailing out.

The drop was near the Scottish National Gallery and we worried that a few tourists might take an interest in what we were doing. The last thing we wanted was for any of them to appear in shot, so Dave set up his camera at the bottom of the slope. My plan was to jump quickly on to the wall and drop down as soon as he gave me the OK.

It was freezing. All I was wearing was a merino-wool base layer, so I rode across a few obstacles to warm up. Despite the chilly temperatures, I was feeling confident because I had been on my bike so much. I also knew that Dave had built up a strong foundation of shots. The Princes Street Gardens stunt might become our banger, if I managed to land it.

I peered over the edge, and Dave gave me a look that I knew meant he was ready. We checked to see who was around. Once it was clear, I got up on to the wall and put my feet on the pedals when something hit me.

My fork's going to snap off, I thought, not knowing where the idea had come from. I just had a gut feeling. I let the doubts pass. So what? At least it'll be on film. Plus, I've been waiting for this for ages . . . I'm gonna go for it.

My fear factor was under control. I had stood at the top of that wall so often, looking down and planning, that I wasn't scared. The line was practical. I was jumping on to something I could see rather than hopping off a blind edge and flipping into the unknown. I dropped off the wall and landed on the ledge before cascading on to the bank. But upon impact with the grass my fork snapped, just as I'd predicted, and I tumbled towards the concrete path below. I was annoyed but unhurt. My next reaction, weirdly, was to laugh. I'd just jumped off the side of a building, but there I was, chuckling at the bottom unscathed.

With my bike in bits, we had to wait for a month before the weather allowed us another shot. And when our chance finally came we prepared in the same way: Dave set up at the bottom and I worked from the wall, this time with mixed results. In the first attempt I slammed my foot on to a gutter, badly bruising my heel in the process. On the second I landed both wheels on the grass bank and cruised to the path, relieved. Princes Street Gardens was by far the biggest thing I'd ridden. It might just be the high point in our film.

Once we had reviewed the clip I felt a slight stab of disappointment. As I'd hopped off, a bunch of tourists had looked over the wall in disbelief. I think they were half expecting to see my body lying in a crumpled heap. Dave was annoyed. We'd wanted our shots to look clean, with no passers-by. It wasn't until much later on, once the film had been released, that we realized those spectators actually worked for us. People could imagine being those tourists looking down, and thinking, *What the heck?!*

Eighty per cent of the filming was done. I had 360'd down the subway stairs near the Sheraton Hotel – all seventeen of them. On another day we filmed a flair off a tree in the Meadows, a big public park in the city. I'd wanted to go upside down in the street for a while, and if you don't know what a flair is, it's a fairly technical stunt where you roll up a transition (or slope) and begin a back-flip motion, before turning your head slightly. That allows you to rotate 180 degrees in the air – in theory. When landing, the rider should be facing back to where they first started.

This style of trick can't be done on just any old tree; the roots in the Meadows were unique and had been known to BMXers for years because they created the perfect ramp. I still needed to do a bit of extra labour for the film, though, and to get the approach just right, I filled in the roots around the base to create a smooth run-up. Crash mats were placed around the landing zone so I could practise without picking up any injuries.

Nobody seemed bothered by what I was doing around

the Meadows, Princes Street Gardens, or on the university campus, and I was always careful not to get under anyone's feet whenever I was slicing about. We kept our work low profile. We were mindful not to attract any crowds, and we only ever got hassle from the occasional security guard. Even our shot over Chuckie Pend passed without incident, or a ticking-off, probably because we were so super-discreet during the preparations. (Well, as discreet as you can be when jumping over two shopfronts on a busy main road.) When it came to filming, one morning Dave and I sized up the roofs while the street was quiet, the pair of us looking around to see who was about. So far we'd completed all our work without running into the police. I wanted it to stay that way.

Once on top, I realized Nash was right. Both roofs had been designed with perfectly flat surfaces. There was enough space to make a decent run-up, too. I told Dave the line was on, and he hoisted up the bike and positioned himself on the other side of the road with his camera, even though I hadn't cleared anything with Colin from Macdonald Cycles. I knew he wouldn't mind. He was usually pretty laid back. And as for those guys at CopyStop? Well, we were better off getting the jump done first. I figured we could ask for forgiveness later – that's if anyone kicked up a fuss. My only real concern was the flats above. It was a Sunday. I didn't want to scare the life out of somebody taking a shower, or settling down for breakfast.

When it came to filming the gap, my first attempt

was pretty loose: I misjudged the distance and overshot the lip, looping out and landing on the roof, backside first. I was lucky not to have rag-dolled it on to the pavement below. The second effort was much easier. I flew over the top, cruised to the end of the CopyStop roof and dropped to the wall below – a distance of around ten feet – hopping on to the street afterwards. In the end, it was such a simple trick that I repeated the jump another five or six times so Dave could get the perfect shot from underneath.

Chuckie Pend was another solid line in the bag and, once we'd finalized nearly every shot, Dave decided that he wanted to match our work with an epic soundtrack, something off-radar and emotive. There was plenty of stuff on his shortlist – Sigur Ros, The Walkmen, among others – but in the end he opted for a heavy ballad called 'The Funeral' by Band of Horses, an indie rock group from Seattle. Dave and me figured our release would be so low key that we wouldn't have to approach any record labels for permission. Neither of us worried that anybody involved with the band was going to see it, either.

In fact, Dave and myself had zero commercial expectations beyond the mountain-bike scene, so when we finalized our five minutes fifty-seven seconds cut it was closed off without a title. Eventually, we settled upon *Inspired Bicycles*, by way of a thank-you for the support Dave Cleaver had given me with parts and prototype equipment. Mentioning sponsors in a video name was the done thing in BMXing. It seemed fitting here, too. With filming completed, I went back to Dunvegan to help Dad as he worked on the roof at the Angus MacAskill Museum, trimming rushes, or reeds, for the thatched lining. I had just left my job at Macdonald Cycles. The Clan had become so popular I didn't need to work during the week, and that meant I was able to pop back to Skye for a few days, no problems.

Once Dave had finished cutting the film we organized a DIY screening for some mates. There was no red carpet, definitely no paparazzi, just beer and crisps from the local offie. We weren't in the mood for a grand unveiling, and we watched *Inspired Bicycles* three times before uploading it on to YouTube. Having worked on it for six months, our premiere felt anticlimactic. We didn't even drink the booze, and as the evening went on there was no real rush to see how people were taking to it online. Besides, *Family Guy* was on the telly.

It wasn't as if anything big was going to happen.

Scene Nine

(<u>EXT.</u>) Marchmont, Edinburgh

Cut to a row of flat-topped metal railings on a quiet Edinburgh street. Danny approaches on his bike, hops up to a nearby electrical box and attempts to ride along a line he has nicknamed 'the spiky fence'. The flat-topped bars are only an inch wide. His front tyre seems unable to find any balance.

On Danny's first attempt, the back wheel slips away and his spokes catch in the railings as he tumbles forward.

<u>FADE OUT</u>

The next time we see Danny, he's using a wooden block to hammer his now-buckled wheel back into shape. He looks frustrated . . .

Inspired Bicycles, 2009

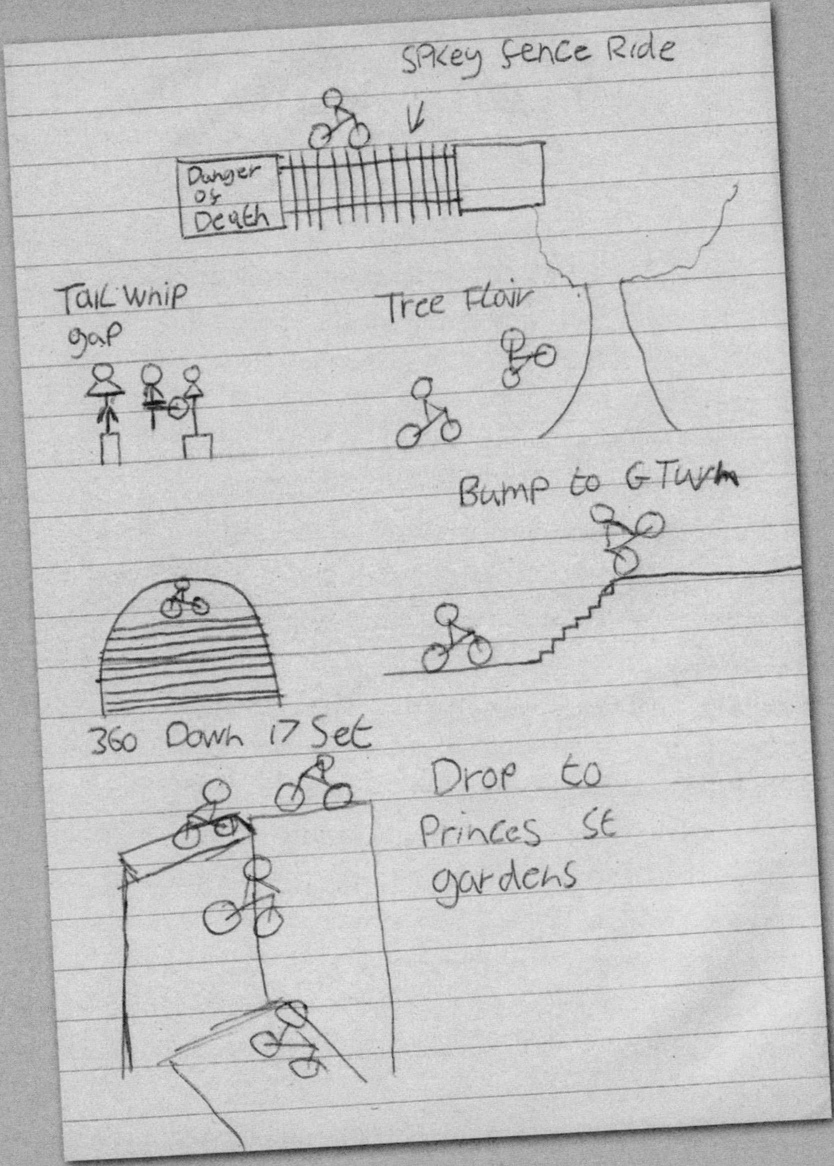

Spikey Fence Ride

Danger
of
Death

Tail whip
gap

Tree Flair

Bump to G Turn

360 Down 17 Set

Drop to
Princes St
gardens

9. Danger of Death! Keep Off!
(The Spiky Fence Story)

Scan through twenty-two seconds of the *Inspired Bicycles* video on YouTube and you'll see it: a five-and-a-half-foot-tall spiky fence made up of smooth, flat-topped poles about six inches apart and no more than a thumb tip in width. The fence was in Marchmont, which was near to the flat, and I'd often ride past it on my way to work. But one morning, just after Dave and I had started shooting, I pulled up for a closer look.

Hmm, I wonder . . . I thought, sizing up the height.

It would be a pretty far-fetched piece of riding to get across on two wheels, but I dropped my bike and clambered up to the electrical box which had been built at one end of the railing. That ledge was my only starting point. To ride over, I would need to cycle about twenty feet to another box that had been built at the end of the spikes.

The City of Edinburgh Council had stuck hazard stickers to the exterior. 'DANGER OF DEATH! KEEP OFF!' Each one was a warning that, should I ever come into contact with the wiring inside, I might end up resembling a badly burnt teacake. But the hazard signs were also a summary of how I felt about the fence itself. I could tell falling off was going to be painful. Still, I rode to Macdonald Cycles on the Wee Commuty, filing Marchmont at the back of my mind as something we should attempt during our next filming session.

Over the following month there were times when I wished I'd never called out that line. The fence was stupidly hard to negotiate and just getting on required a lot of luck. The smallest amount of moisture on the metal would reduce any grip to zero, causing my wheels to slip down one side of the bars, my limbs the other. After two hours of trying on the first day, the risks were obvious. By falling off, face first, there was a real chance that I might become the latest scene on an emergency-services reality-TV show, having been impaled on the metal.

There was also the issue of authenticity. Apart from my jump over Chuckie Pend (where I had to ladder it up to the shopfront of Macdonald Cycles before riding over two shop doorways), I didn't have any climbing in the video. I had wanted everything to be doable on the bike, from the ground up, and my jumping on to ledges and rails became an obsession. The spiky fence was no different. I had to build a little wooden bump at the bottom of the electrical box as a base, and from there I could hop to the top on my wheels.

We spent days trying to nail the shot. Often, success seemed impossible. Holding a line across those spikes was probably the hardest trick I've ever done; just levelling up the front wheel with the top of the railing was terrifying. Once

I'd moved forward, bringing my back wheel into position, the poles became even scarier. I felt exposed. I'd slip. I'd tip forward. Whenever I had done skinnies previously, I often got a feeling I was going to pull it off just as I approached the end. It could be tempting to celebrate before getting there. This was different. There were too many occasions when I was a foot or two from the finish, only for my front or back wheel to slip, right at the death. It was so frustrating.

For hours I hopped on to the electrical box and tried to negotiate those rails, over and over in the freezing cold. By the end of every session, Dave would be shivering, his lips blue, but he never got disheartened. After a couple of days of crashes and spills, I'd endured enough. Dave had endured enough. We took a break, promising to try again in a few weeks and I went back to Macdonald Cycles after the last session, feeling pretty discouraged. I'd experienced real failure on my bike for the first time ever. I also worried that our chances were blown. Winter was coming in and the trick was weather-dependent. We needed dry conditions for the wheels to stick.

Sometimes, a stunt can become a psychological hurdle as well as a physical one – for me, anyway. And weirdly, it's not always the hardest stunts that bring the toughest challenges. Like when I was making the *Imaginate* video in 2012: I wanted to pull a flair off a ramp made from four giant playing cards, the one in front being the five of diamonds (which is now my *least* favourite in the deck). It was the last shot on the schedule, and one of the less challenging on paper, but it soon became my nemesis. I would ride up to the ramp and pull away; I spent hours and hours and hours circling around the cards in an attempt to settle myself. I just couldn't finish the flair and I genuinely considered scrapping the idea. In the end we wasted nearly four days before I managed to land it, a problem I put down to brain freeze, or a mental hiccup.

The spiky fence in my *Inspired Bicycles* video was different. Rather than a psychological hurdle, it was just a pain in the arse. When we returned, I could sense the end was in reach because of all the practice I'd been doing. But I was still losing my balance halfway along and, having spent three days on the spikes, I felt done. I didn't want to face it again. Dave had other ideas, though, and one night in the flat he told me to give it one more go.

I wasn't so sure, but I knew Dave: he wasn't one for pushing a rider into the impossible. I decided to give it another shot, and when a blue-sky day next came around we rode back to Marchmont. It was April. The air was cold but the ground was dry and, with my back wheel lined up on the fence, I could sense a result. As I edged forward, my balance wobbled; I had to hang out a leg in a desperate attempt to stay stable. Finally, I rode both wheels to the end.

Getting there felt odd. There was no celebration or sense of euphoria. I was stoked, but nailing a big trick is an unusual experience. There's no adrenaline at the end, and very little exhilaration. Instead, the emotion I go through the most is relief, rather than happiness – relief at finally completing a challenge that has put me into a mental spin for so long.

Scene Ten

(<u>INT.</u>) An indoor gymnasium.

Pro flatlander BMX rider Keelan Phillips pirouettes on his bike, his wheels gliding around the polished floor.

VOICEOVER: Street sports used to happen out of sight. In places we don't care about, underground sports in ignored spaces. But something just changed.

(<u>EXT.</u>) Various street scenes.

Cut to skateboarders and free runners in the street. Next there's a part from Inspired Bicycles: it's Danny. He's in the Meadows, flaring off a tree.

VOICEOVER: Viral videos have been around for well over a decade. But a new wave of films has begun to emerge showcasing the talents of a new generation of street-sport stars. These supposedly niche sports have found a massive and willing mainstream audience online. Who'd have thought tens of millions of people would ever care about parkour, skateboarding or trials bikes?

Cut to another clip of Danny from Inspired Bicycles. This time he's jumping the gap at Chuckie Pend.

VOICEOVER: One of these sports is urban trial riding. Biking over unlikely street obstacles without putting a foot down, in competition with other riders. But it wasn't competitive success that rapidly brought one rider global acclaim . . .

Later, the camera cuts to Danny. This time he's standing by a red telephone box in Dunvegan.

DANNY: It's been a very odd journey. I was back here last week cutting the peats across the hills there. Then I go off and do other (things) . . . it's almost like two different worlds.

Concrete Circus, Channel 4, 2011

10. Outbreak

Everything changed the next morning: 20 April 2009 – a Monday. I was asleep when my mobile vibrated on the bedside table.

'Hello, is that Danny?' said an unknown voice.

I checked the screen; the number had been withheld. 'Yeah . . . who's this?'

'Oh, great! I'm from the BBC, and we've seen your video. We'd love to interview you about it . . .'

I didn't respond at first. I couldn't work it out. Maybe someone was trying to wind me up. Then the penny dropped: were they talking about *Inspired Bicycles*? There was an outside chance that somebody *might* have seen it, but that seemed unlikely. The video had only gone online the night before. I mumbled some excuse about having to 'get ready' and hung up, calling out to Dave. I wanted to check YouTube on his laptop. I wasn't that fussed about the figures, but if people were hooking into it and the BBC had spotted us, well, we might have already found some traction within the trials scene.

When Dave logged on, we saw that hundreds of thousands

of people had already watched *Inspired Bicycles*; there were comments from viewers all over the world. The volume was unbelievable, and the chatter was largely positive. I read messages from trials bikers and BMXers, kids and older riders. The TV presenter, comedian and writer Stephen Fry mentioned the video on Twitter, as did former Tour de France champ Lance Armstrong, then still the biggest name in the cycling world, pre-disgrace.

This all meant very little. I wasn't dialled in to social media, I didn't own a laptop, and the whole concept of You-Tube and Twitter was new to me. I rarely expanded my horizons beyond the bike scene. I didn't have a clue about the internet. The other thing was that in 2009, nobody really watched videos on their mobiles and the iPhone phenom-enon was only just beginning. Virals weren't a concept.

Anyway, *Inspired Bicycles* wasn't made for the hype. We did it because we wanted to do something that riders could appreci-ate in their homes, just like *Grounded* and *Chainspotting*. I certainly hadn't got involved out of any ambition to be a pro cyclist, because I was more into the idea of becoming a mechanic on the World Cup race circuit. As far as I could tell, there wasn't any money to be made from trials, not outside of shows, but to be frank, I never rode my bike to make money. There were, however, the lucky few who had broken into the mainstream: Martyn Ashton, Hans Rey and Chris Akrigg. They were operating in a different stratosphere.

The attention snowballed. National newspapers called me at home. There were crazy requests from companies wanting to discuss sponsorship deals – energy drinks, bike manufacturers, clothing brands. I ignored it all and kept riding with the Clan. I was wary of jumping on any kind of bandwagon. Then, one day when I was sitting with Dave in his car, my phone rang. It was a producer from *The Ellen DeGeneres Show*, an American chat show presented by the comic of the same name. In a surreal phone call, the producer offered me a cameo role on their programme, which they assured me was prime time.

'We'd love you to race through the streets of Chicago, dressed as Ellen,' they explained. 'Maybe you can jump over some walls and do a stunt off a bus stop, or even a phone box?'

I tried to hold back a laugh. I'm a rider . . . I thought. *Nah*. It didn't sound credible.

The producer tried to convince me by explaining that at least one US president had appeared on the show, and that my appearance would be tongue-in-cheek. But I wasn't fussed. I politely said, 'Thanks, but no thanks,' and wished them good luck. I had no idea who Ellen DeGeneres was.

Even saying 'no' caused problems. Once the papers had found out, turning down *The Ellen DeGeneres Show* created a series of headlines in its own right, and not just in the UK. My half-sister Mary was in San Diego at the time. She rang me, shocked, having seen a newspaper article featuring the story of her little brother and his mate riding around Edinburgh with a video camera. A wee while later, some friends were on holiday in New Zealand. As they queued for buns in a bakery, they overheard a couple talking about *Inspired Bicycles*. It was all so strange. Meanwhile, there were more and more articles being written, and Mum had started filling a shoebox with clippings that mentioned me. Before too long it was over-flowing (until some mice got in one night and ate the lot).

The fuss seemed totally mad, and my head could have been turned, especially by some of the offers on the table, but my aim was to remain authentic. During the making of *Inspired Bicycles* I had wanted to show off trials riding. Now, because of Dave's camera, a spotlight had been shone on a scene that hadn't got that much attention before – not in the mainstream world, like BMX or mountain biking had. I was determined to keep the momentum going, but only if the work presented my riding in the right way. Anything cheesy was out. So, dressing up as a female TV chat-show host while riding through Chicago? *No thanks*. I also turned down the chance to do a half-time gig at the Scottish FA Cup Final because I had already committed to performing at a small agricultural gala with the Clan. Those decisions alone probably summed up how I was feeling about all this new attention.

I'd turn to Dave for advice. Whenever an invitation came through, or a sponsor offered me a commercial contract, I'd check in with him. I wanted to make sure that everything I did arrived with the highest level of integrity. He was tuned in to what had worked before in BMX and made his sugges-tions. With the limited things I agreed to, such as an interview with *The New York Times*, I talked everything through with Dave first. I didn't want to sell myself out, or the scene. Had I taken on everything that was pushed my way, I would have probably made a nice chunk of money and travelled the world five times over. The flipside is that I might not have lasted as long as a professional film-maker, or become as creatively free as I am now.

My MO was pretty basic: I simply did what I thought was right, while believing everything would work out for the best.

My attitude to all of this was: *Why me?* Prior to the release of *Inspired Bicycles*, there had been some amazing riding parts released online, but our wee film seemed to catch everybody's imagination. We had come out of nowhere and, as the attention around us got bigger and more intense, I realized that most internet successes were clips of cats playing pianos, or somebody falling off a ladder. *Inspired Bicycles* was different. We had produced something quality-controlled which had been six months in the making.

We were shooting in an unusual style for a riding film, too. There had been some amazing videos in sports such as BMX or skateboarding, but those guys were doing stuff that was so technically insane it was hard for viewers to get their heads around what it was they were seeing. The camera work and riding were impressive, but they didn't seem to translate well to mainstream audiences. Riders were doing rail grinds, or switch tricks, which everyday folk were unable to relate to.

That's what I loved so much about Ruben's section in *Grounded*. He rode everything on two wheels, no pegs, over everyday street furniture like stair sets, walls and railings. It was the same for us in *Inspired Bicycles*. People who wouldn't have ordinarily watched a riding film picked up on the simplicity of my lines – like the tree in the Meadows, the spiky fence in Marchmont, or the shop doorways over Macdonald Cycles – and got a kick out of them. Every stunt was tangible; people could relate to the objects because they passed similar things on their way to work – subway steps, a gate, a shop doorway. Just as important were the shock moments, such as at Princes Street Gardens, where it looked like I was jumping off the edge of a building. Those clips created a powerful emotion – disbelief, shock, fear – so the temptation to share them online was pretty high.

Inspired Bicycles also made big waves in the cycling world. It was talked up in the trials and mountain-bike scenes because nobody had put that much time and effort into a street video before. Even the BMXers liked it because they could appreciate how Dave had edited the film, as well as the tricks on show. Later, one of my heroes, Hans Rey, hyped me up on Twitter. 'Damn, check this out,' he wrote a week after its release. He described *Inspired Bicycles* as being on 'a whole new level'. Now, that was something I *could* get excited about.

There was an even bigger shock on the way: in May 2009, Martyn Ashton, my riding hero, called up to invite me on to his Animal Bike Tour – a trials road show featuring some of the best riders on the planet, and one of my inspirations for starting the Clan. The performance was taking place at the BikeRadar Live Show in Donington Park, and I was stoked. We had been doing great things around Scotland, but the Animal Bike Tour was a huge deal. Everything was bigger. The organizers were renowned for getting top names, like

Martyn and Sam Pilgrim, who went on to become the FMB World Tour Champion.

Martyn and Co. always attracted huge crowds, and the Animal tour was often booked in for riding's biggest events, like the Goodwood Festival of Speed and the MotoGP. Their displays were also the benchmark for any trials display team in Britain, if not the world, because of the size and scale of tricks involved. Unsurprisingly, I was a bit intimidated at first. This was the BikeRadar Live Show, the biggest cycling festival in Britain. When Martyn came by to say hello, I was overwhelmed, even though he was super-enthusiastic about *Inspired Bicycles*. Looking around, the posters from my bedroom wall in Dunvegan were coming to life. Hans Rey was in the crowd, as was Steve Peat and Brian Lopes. *Insane.*

The crowds were bigger than any I had been used to with the Clan, and I had a fair amount of hype to live up to that day, but I wasn't stressed. I felt physically great. I was in the best form of my life because I'd been on the bike all year, doing some of the hardest lines I'd ever attempted. I felt strong, and every jump and gap I worked into my routine came off easily. I also felt comfortable within Animal's set-up – the boxes, the ramps and the rails. I knew I could deliver on the big stage and, as I tyre-tapped off the top of a Winnebago bus at the close of the show, I realized I'd nailed it.

The Animal show was something I'd admired from afar. After doing a performance in front of all my heroes, I felt like I was being accepted into the mountain-bike world.

*

People in the streets spotted me on my bike and wanted to stop and talk. In Edinburgh I would find myself chatting to Japanese and American tourists about the video; some had even come to Edinburgh *because* of the video.

The only people who weren't that excited (initially) by the fuss surrounding *Inspired Bicycles* were the rock group Band of Horses, songwriters of our unofficial soundtrack. Their single 'The Funeral' had given my riding an emotive vibe, but there was a problem. Because Dave and myself weren't that online savvy, neither of us knew about usage rights. The internet seemed like a free-for-all. Nobody knew what was going on with things like music clearance and copyright. We'd bypassed the correct procedures because we hadn't known what they were (and we didn't think the film would get noticed). But once the video had made a splash, the record label Sub Pop quickly got in touch. They weren't happy. They asked us to take the whole thing down: 'The Funeral', our images, everything.

We panicked. There were stressful emails between record-label types and ourselves. But amidst the wrangling, somebody in the Sub Pop camp noticed that 'The Funeral' had been enjoying an upsurge in unit sales. *Inspired Bicycles* was acting as a promo for the band and people were buying the track. There was a truce. An under-the-table agreement took place. It was a serious lesson.

Dave's filming and my riding might have drawn admiring glances but, when it came to the internet, we were on a steep learning curve.

Scene Eleven

(<u>INT.</u>) DISC Sports & Spine Center, Marina del Rey, California

Danny sits in a treatment room. A specialist assesses the extent of his injuries, by flexing him at the knees and checking for any unusual sensations. With each painful reflex, Danny nods. He looks uncomfortable.

Experts assess scans of his knee. They turn to Danny and explain his options: physio and regular exercise is one, though the niggling pains will remain. The other is surgery. The chance of ending the problem is put at '90 plus per cent'.

Danny seems unsure of what to do.

MacAskill's Imaginate, Episode 1, 2013

Immediate Regret

AWEEEE!!...

11. On the Boulevard of Broken Bones

By the end of the year the offers had piled up; my life was a bit of a blur. In one day, there were requests from people in ten countries – more TV producers asked me to appear on their shows, documentary makers wanted interviews and record labels wanted me for videos. Because of the viral's title, a lot of requests were coming through to Dave at Inspired Bicycles, which must have driven him mad. He was forced to set up a Danny MacAskill email address where people could leave their business requests. It hardly helped. I didn't have a laptop. Every time I logged on to a mate's computer, or visited an internet café, my inbox was overflowing.

The video trailed me everywhere. If I did a show with the Clan, people wanted to talk about *Inspired Bicycles*, so I needed someone to handle the workload. As I trawled through my emails, I noticed interested parties had offered to represent me. Some of them were more mainstream than I would have liked – sports agencies that handled tennis players, golfers and pro track or road cyclists. Others were skilled in representing high-end athletes in the extreme-sports world – snowboarders, BMXers and skaters. I was keen to remain in the mountain-bike and trials scene, so there was only one option: Tarek Rasouli.

Tarek had been a star in freeriding and BMX until a 2002 injury left him in a wheelchair. He had been shooting the *Kranked V* DVD in Sun Peaks, British Columbia, when a jump went horribly wrong. Tarek damaged his spine in the fall but, hopefully, with advancements in technology, my friend will one day walk again. I'd seen his videos and read several interviews with him in the mountain-bike mags. From the way he talked, I'd imagined him as a formidable character.

Tarek represented some big names on the scene, including the Red Bull-sponsored mountain bikers Andreu Lacondeguy and Martin Söderström. Those guys were the pinnacle of freeride mountain biking. Signing with Tarek and his management company, Rasoulution, seemed the perfect choice. He was somebody who could bring a little organization and business savvy without it affecting my integrity.

We began sorting the good offers from the bad. Tarek was about the hardest-working person I'd met and I would field calls from him at all kinds of ungodly hours. He was channelling as much energy into his management work as he had with his pro career. Tarek is a force of nature.

We were quickly working from the same page. I told him about my need for authenticity and my fear of signing any contract that might damage my reputation. One of the first things he became aware of was the fact that I wasn't driven by money. 'I'm not into fancy sports cars or anything like that,' I told him at one of our early meetings. 'It's not what makes me tick.' It's the same today. I'm still living in a Glasgow flat with seven mates. The rent isn't much more than £250 a month. Maybe I'll buy a house at some point, but for now I'm happy. Tarek got my attitude straightaway.

'But I'm not stupid,' I added. 'I realize I can't do this for ever, so it would be pretty cool to come out of my riding career with a decent set-up so I can have some creative freedom for later on . . .'

There was also my position within the mountain-bike world to figure out. Trials was a niche group within a collection of sports that included downhill, cross country and dirt jumping – even the people around the country who rode their bicycles at weekends. Mountain biking wasn't as militant as some of the other sports such as BMX, or skateboarding. It was accepting of all riders.

Trials was considered part of the family because it had developed from mountain biking. Back in the early days of the Kamikaze Bike Games, an annual mountain-bike event held in Mammoth, California, competitors would race on the slopes in a downhill heat. They would later compete in trials during the same event, and that's where Hans Rey made his name. He had brought trials into the mainstream

1. Riding on Port Charlotte beach, Isle of Islay, 1993.

2. Me and younger sister Margaret Ishbel, delighted with our new wheels.

3. Me and wee sister in wheelbarrow wheeled by Dad in Dunvegan.

4. Me thatching the Giant Angus MacAskill Museum roof.

5. Tyre-tapping tree in the Meadows: filming for *Inspired Bicycles*, Edinburgh, 2009.

6. Spiky fence-ride in Marchmont, Edinburgh, April 2009.

7. Gap from MacDonald Cycles roof to copy shop, Edinburgh, 2009.

8. Gap from wall ride to drop at the Scottish National Gallery into Princes Street Gardens, Edinburgh.

9. Back flip off driftwood,
Arisaig beach, Scotland.

10. Tyre-tapping old
iron-mine foundation
on Raasay, filming for
Way Back Home, 2010.

11. Bunny-hop front-flipping off an old water tank above Dunvegan, 2010.

12. *From right to left:* Dave Sowerby, Mark Huskisson, me. Camping out at Arisaig while filming *Way Back Home*, 2010.

13. Curry night in the *Way Back Home* camper, me and Dave, 2010.

through those competitions, although it still operated on the fringes because the techniques required to be successful were so ridiculously hard to master.

So I was a niche figure within a niche scene. I stood alone. I'd made one video and had gathered a lot of attention quickly and accidentally. There were other riders who were making videos and earning a good living, like Chris Akrigg, but they were few and far between. (Chris had also been filming for a long time and his production standards were high. Whenever he released a new title it always made waves.)

Tarek understood that I was a unique challenge and, in his head, we were taking a big jump into the unknown. Not that I cared too much. I couldn't believe how lucky I was.

As far as sponsors went, Red Bull seemed like the perfect home. The energy drink had long been a supporter of extreme-sports events. They also had an impressive roster of athletes who were paid to wear their hats, helmets or T-shirts, while competing in comps like X-Games, or during riding edits. The list was pretty diverse. There were skiers, moto-cross bikers and surfers. The Athertons, a downhill mountain-bike family, comprising the siblings Rachel, Dan and Gee, were on their books, as was the extreme motorcyclist Robbie Maddison. Tarek figured Red Bull would be keen on my style.

I'd first got wind that they were interested in bringing me on board before I signed with Tarek. I met with some of the athlete managers after an email conversation following the success of *Inspired Bicycles*, but I had the feeling they might not be too crazy about trials, mainly because of its niche appeal. They also might have been asking themselves whether I was going to be a one-hit wonder. Yeah, *Inspired Bicycles* had been a success, but could I do it again? I had set the bar pretty high, after all. I was wondering the same thing. We had put six months into its making, in a city I'd been riding a while. Could I do something new, and fresh, in a shorter space of time?

Plenty of assessment presumably went on in that first meeting. A lot of what Red Bull did with its athletes was based on personality as well as ability, and their roster featured larger-than-life characters. The hope was that Red Bull would give me the opportunity to put together a follow-up to *Inspired Bicycles*. In return, I would wear one of their branded helmets, which was the mark of being one of the top folk in any extreme sport.

'I wanna make a film with my friends, someone like Dave, who worked on *Inspired* . . .' I told them. 'And I want to use the music I like.' I was keen to do everything on my own terms and, to my surprise, Red Bull agreed. They even had a new concept for me to think about.

'How about you take a Scottish road trip, Danny?' the athlete manager suggested. 'You could start in Edinburgh and drive all the way to Skye, stopping off at some great destinations along the way.'

That suggestion ticked all the boxes. I knew I could showcase what I'd considered to be the real Scotland, the beautiful and remote rural areas that not a lot of people got to see. From there I could perform street trials, lines by the lochs, front flips from old ruins in the Highlands. I could even finish with some tricks around my old haunts in Dunvegan. I was fired up.

With an agreement with Red Bull now in place, Tarek decided I should focus on some of the other offers that had been sitting in my email inbox. Prior to signing with Rasoulution, I'd already filmed a music video for the indie rock band Doves ('Winter Hill') and an advert with recruitment company S.1. Jobs, in which I performed tricks around Edinburgh and Aberdeen, including another tree flair. The idea behind the video was fairly simple: if you managed to get a job that you loved, commuting could be a joy. I was dressed in a suit and tie for the filming, which, in hindsight, seemed pretty apt. Trials and Tarek had set me up with a dream career.

But disaster struck. Well, not so much disaster, more an occupational hazard for a rider. In August 2009 I had travelled to California with Tarek to meet a new sponsor or two, which included a day in San Diego at the HQ of sunglasses manufacturer Oakley. Their offices were a bit of a playground, and I was given free rein to muck about. The owner had a decommissioned tank that we were allowed to drive; I even got to ride along the top, which was pretty surreal.

Later, I was shown to a cool little pump track at the back of the building, a rolling dirt trail of berms (banked turns on a dirt course). A cyclist doesn't have to use the pedals once they're slicing around a pump track. Just the motion of moving up and down on the bike, or 'pumping' the back side of a transition, is enough to cruise around. For a while I was cutting about the trail and even tried a few flips out of the berms. When drifting through the dust at the bottom of the track I suddenly lost my front end. As I hit the ground, the fall snapped my collarbone in two. In theory, it was the simplest form of riding I'd done for the past year, but some-how I'd given myself a serious injury.*

I was out of action for nearly twelve months. After nine weeks of recuperation, I slipped over in Edinburgh while messing around with friends. *Snap!* I felt the bone in my shoulder cracking in two again as I landed. An operation was needed to seam the shattered pieces together and a metal plate was inserted over the break to hold it in place. While in hospital, I could tell the doctors assessing my injury were worried about me getting back on the bike too quickly. They were familiar with my thick medical file. Some of them had even seen my videos. I'm guessing their attitude was:

---

* Typically, it's the small things that get you. Stubbing and breaking your toe on the doorframe; slicing a tendon with a sharp knife while cooking; slipping on a wet bathroom floor and breaking your wrist; and, obviously, losing my front end when riding around an easy pump track. I worry about everyday risks more than riding a high ledge. I think it is to do with concentration. When I'm doing a risky trick, I'm 100 per cent focused. I'm not always on my A game while handling a knife or cutting about the flat in my pants.

Well, we don't want to be responsible for this bloke breaking himself again too soon. Let's be ultra-cautious . . .

This time, I was determined to relax. Apart from an unpleasant infection, my recovery ran pretty smoothly. (It was my own fault: at a party I had climbed into my friend's super-sized fish tank and fully submerged myself. I don't want to think about what had leaked into the surgical incision.) Even though I was getting itchy feet, I rested for what felt like an age and, once I'd got the all-clear to ride in January 2010, I flew back out to California to hang with the Athertons. I stayed on Newport Beach with Red Bull's specialist trainer Darren 'Conehead' Roberts. The plan was to do some training and rehab on my shoulder. It was obvious that I would be a little rusty, so I took my Inspired over to get into the swing of things, but I hardly got out. California was experiencing their worst weather for fifteen years and the whole place seemed about to fall to pieces. By Scottish standards, they were experiencing a little drizzle, nothing more, though it was still enough to cause landslides.

With the Athertons around, I had plenty to keep me distracted. Dan was readying himself for the Olympics, which were a couple of years away. BMX, which he also competed in, had been included among the cycling events and Dan was keen to qualify. Meanwhile, Rachel had just come back from an injury. All of us were itching to get on our bikes.

'Fancy riding some downhill, Danny?' suggested Gee one day. 'We'll sort you out with a bike, no problem.'

I was keen. So for the next few days, a group of us worked our way around the local runs. It was fun, if a little tricky. I'd never been on a downhill bike before and, because of its slack geometry, everything seemed sluggish. The frame was designed for flat-out speed but, once I had the hang of it, I was soon on Gee's tail. Given that he was a multi-World-Cup-winning racer, I was going fast. Probably way too fast. There's no doubt I was punching above my weight.

One afternoon, as we were making our way home, Gee pointed out that the Southridge USA race was coming up in nearby Fontana. 'It's a cool comp,' he said. 'Anyone can enter. You should come along for a laugh.'

I was tempted. The course was well known in California and, while it wasn't *the* place to ride, it was considered a tough course by downhillers. The trail started off on a rocky stretch; at the top it was exposed to the elements and there was a horrible flat section to pedal through at the bottom. But I'd been pleased with how I'd taken to the downhill bike, so I figured, Why not?

In hindsight, quitting while I was ahead would have been the smarter play, though, as Mum could tell you, I've never done that. I was right on the tail of Gee during a practice run when we turned into a rock garden. Suddenly, I clipped a large stone and lost control, flipping over the handlebars for what felt like ten feet. I could see my crash site zooming into view: a nasty-looking rock with my name written all over it.

Oh for goodness' sake, I thought.

I landed straight on my collarbone and felt the all-too-familiar snap of its length being cracked in two.

Anger burned through the pain. I'd been off the bike for six months already – *How long would I be out for now?* I knew that I wasn't under the pressure of deadlines, not like Dan. He had expectations of reaching the Olympics. Great race results were vital to him that year, and the next, so there was some pressure to push ahead. I didn't have any of that, but I still felt sick about it. Red Bull had offered to help me realize the project of a lifetime, and I was eager to start as quickly as possible. It was so frustrating.

I wheeled down to the bottom in a mood. I had been broken in America – again. Now my planned follow-up to *Inspired Bicycles* seemed further away than ever.

Scene Twelve

(<u>EXT.</u>) Edinburgh Castle

Cut to the spires of the city from a distance, followed by the sight of Danny carrying his bike up the castle stairs. The camera pans past a metal field gun.

The next time we see him, Danny is wearing his Red Bull helmet for the first time. He rides around the battlements on his bike.

<u>FADE OUT/IN</u>

Danny stands on a stone wall. Below him is a twelve-foot drop on to a grass slope that feeds on to a concrete path. He peers down, as if assessing the distances. There is apprehension, but only a little. Ahead of him, the city stretches out into the distance . . .

Way Back Home, 2010

Gap to copy shop

MACDonald cycles   COPY SHOP

Bank gap   Wallride to Nose Pick

Wall Ride 180 Ledge   Big Drop

12. Eat the Bigger Frog First

Being banged about had some upsides: I could scope out the locations for my new film, one that we were calling *Way Back Home*. It seemed an apt title for a road trip from Edinburgh to Dunvegan. The idea was to take my street trials into the middle of nowhere, where I could perform a series of tricks on unusual obstacles. The research became a nice distraction from my recuperation time on the sofa. I was bored, and a little grouchy. Aside from the sling holding my arm in place, there was also a pressing medical reason not to get back on the bike. If I had another smash, there was a wee chance the metal plate holding my collarbone together might buckle, slicing my jugular in two.

While lazing around, I experienced something of a technological revolution. I finally bought a laptop and spent hours and hours seeking out cool locations on Google Images. Old castles, disused iron mines, rolling mountains – my mind went into overdrive as I scanned page after page of photos. The requirement for every location was very simple. Every line had to have an amazing backdrop, while vaguely hanging off a route that we'd mapped out on an *A–Z*, from Edinburgh to Skye. I also wanted a series of man-made objects positioned in front of beautiful settings. I even became obsessed with the idea of finding an old red telephone box to jump off. When I checked, there were around 3,500 in Scotland. I must have visited fifty of them until I eventually found the perfect one, which just happened to be on Skye.

Whenever I could, I'd visit the locations myself. I wanted to get a real sense for the lines before I committed to a setting, and I borrowed a mate's old automatic Fiesta to get around. A lot of time was spent driving up and down the country, piecing together a story in my head. Eventually, by June 2010, I was fit enough to ride again, but getting back on my Inspired was tough work. I wasn't fit and my core strength had been shot to pieces. Because of the busted collarbone, tensing my abdominals had been nearly impossible – it was just too painful – and I'd spent nine months rolling around, flopping in and out of bed, or heaving myself out of a sitting position with one arm. I wasn't dialled in.

The ambition was there, though, and after some limited work on the Inspired, Red Bull announced they were going to give me a camper van for the project. That way, Dave Sowerby and myself could have a portable hotel as we rode around the country. When it arrived, I couldn't believe my luck. The mobile home was a 1996 Fiat Royale Sandemere, and it arrived in pristine condition. It must have been the previous owners' pride and joy, and it was perfect for what we were doing. I could strap two bikes to the back and a load of crash mats on the roof. Inside, there was space to sleep six, but only three of us would be using the beds – Dave, myself and a mate called Mark Huskisson, who was documenting the film-making process. Talk about luxury. By the time I'd fitted two twelve-inch sub speakers inside and a disco ball to the ceiling, it was home.

Despite their generous present, Red Bull's involvement was limited. There wasn't a crazy budget, but that meant the creative control on *Way Back Home* was ours. We had free rein to do whatever we wanted, and we were pretty ambitious. My aim was to match the images and riding of *Inspired Bicycles* and I made plans to cruise across the railing on Skye Bridge before dropping off the side and into the sea, which was around a hundred feet below; we talked about scaling the Inaccessible Pinnacle, the notoriously treacherous mountain ridge that dominated the Skye horizon. There was even some chat about getting a helicopter. As we thrashed out lines and locations, I kept saying to Dave, 'What's the best thing I can do on my bike, and where would be the coolest place to do it?'

For years, I'd quite fancied doing something across the Edinburgh Castle battlements. Whenever I cycled around the bottom in Princes Street Gardens, I would stare up and imagine the great old building's potential. There was a long stone wall at the top, which overlooked a steep grass bank and, from there, a tyre-tap, downside 360 tailwhip seemed possible. I reckoned I could make it down without rag-dolling to the path at the base of the incline. But the dream was a tyre-tap front flip off the same wall.

After two weeks of shooting and some long days featuring plenty of hard riding across the islands of Firth and Forth, I put in a few calls to the communications team at Edinburgh Castle. Unbelievably, we were granted access to the wall for ninety minutes. A surreal vibe hit the van as we drove along the Royal Mile, through the gates of the castle and into a cavern of blasted rock. When we entered the bowels of the main building, it was like driving into the Bat Cave.

Our secluded surroundings probably gave us a false sense of security. Outside, it was blowing a hoolie. Once we'd climbed to the top of the wall, the three of us were attacked by the elements. We stood with our shoulders shrugged and hoods up, the cold rain lashing at our backs. I couldn't imagine getting any footage in those conditions. A health-and-safety officer, a real Alan Partridge type in high-vis gear, had arrived to check the wind speeds: any gusts over 50mph, he said, and we'd have to end our shooting. It was much too dangerous to stand on the battlements, let alone hop across them.

Everybody gathered around a monitor as the numbers flickered between 45mph and 48mph. Dave glanced across. His look said: Best get on with it, Danny, and I began warming up with a few 360 nose-taps over the wall. The wind wasn't affecting me at all, but the landing surface was hell-ish. The grass was slippery, everything was muddy, but I was still able to run a few tricks smoothly. That's when I figured I should take a chance.

Well, if I'm only gonna get up here once, I thought, the dream would be to front-flip off the wall and on to the bank below . . .

As a stunt, it was uncharted territory for me. I'd previously landed a bunny-hop front flip on two wheels while rolling down Aberdour Beach in Fife, but landing a tyre-tap front flip on to a sodden slope was a whole other ball game. The idea felt like madness in the rain and howling wind. But there was one chance: I knew I'd be able to get my head around the jump if I could flip on to some crash mats first. That way I could land safely as I assessed the technique needed to force my body weight over the handlebars – my back brake locked – and on to the bank twelve feet below.

Everything felt alien. As I waited at the top, bouncing on my back wheel and holding the tyre over the edge, the slope seemed miles away. I don't know about this, I thought, peer-ing down, before hurling myself over, the momentum propelling my bike in a near-circle as I landed into the mats, backside first. It wasn't perfect, but it was a miracle I'd landed at all, rather than face-planting it in a muddy slide to the bottom. I was nearly there.

Hold on, I thought. This could work.

I walked back to the top, where, after a few botched attempts, I made the solid landing, my tyres hitting the mat in an impact that chucked me over the handlebars. I couldn't believe it. I'd gazed up at that wall for so long and dreamt of flipping over the top. Now I felt there was a chance this could actually work.

Not that I was in great shape. I was cold, wet and tired. I was also feeling pretty beat up after a fortnight of solid riding, and my mental capacity to deal with it had been worn down. Our time was running out, and the health-and-safety dude with his clock and wind meter was making himself extremely busy. We had also drawn a modest crowd. In the café above, a bunch of German tourists had gathered and were staring and pointing through the glass. It wasn't long before all of them were aiming their cameras towards us. Dave stressed that one of our attempts might leak on to YouTube and our work would be blown.

When dealing with fear, I could be easily distracted. I sometimes got caught up in a mental grapple while readying myself for a jump or a flip. Even if everything around me had been shut off on those battlements and it had been just a ledge, the slope below and my bike, I would have endured a hard time getting my body to make that initial jump. But with a few other distracting factors chucked in, like camera positions, a hoolie and camera-wielding German tourists in Pac-a-macs, my job had become even harder.

Without the mats, I was able to nail the flip first time around. I was stoked, but Dave had missed the shot. He was livid about it, though it must have been pretty uncomfortable for him up there. He had been watching in the freezing cold as I'd psyched myself up. The pair of us had been working for an hour, and a lot of that time had involved me peering over the edge of the wall, preparing to jump. But Dave understood my processes. He knew I was unable to change the way I approached a jump. It would have been nice if I could have just thrown myself off the Edinburgh Castle edge – no doubts, no second thoughts – but the fear was there. What I was about to do was dangerous. I had to work through it as sensibly, and as rationally, as I could.

As I readied myself for another attempt, I thought back to a piece of advice I'd once heard in the past. Somebody had told me, 'If you have a frog to eat, don't sit and stare at it – eat. And if you've got two frogs to eat, eat the bigger one first.' It was a roundabout way of saying, *If there's something horrible to be done, better to get it done quickly.* But that idea had rarely worked for me. Some riders have the capability to say, 'Right, there's no point in stressing, just go at it.' But I tended to sit and stare at the frog for a long time. The frog always stared back. Then, after nearly an hour, I was ready . . .

I dropped my front wheel off the edge, throwing my body over the handlebars and pulling the back wheel around my head in the same movement. For a split second, I spun through the air, my tyres biting into the turf as I landed. Despite the wet surface, I was able to maintain balance, cruising to the bottom and skidding to a halt on the concrete path. I couldn't quite believe it. I'd landed one of my dream tricks on camera. Even better, I felt like I was breaking barriers in the trials world.

The worry and frustration of staring at that frog had been worth it.

We criss-crossed Scotland for months, seeking out locations. Originally, the making of *Way Back Home* was supposed to last no more than a few weeks. It took us five months to complete. The camper van covered 17,000 miles and on some days it felt as if we were peeing in the wind with our shooting schedule. Certain parts would take days to get right. Others would come together, only for the weather to turn. We'd chase the sun, which was pretty hard to do in Scotland. There would be other days where I'd work for six hours straight, unable to finish a line.

Every night I would end up spooning the two twelve-inch sub speakers that had been stashed alongside me. When morning came Dave would get up and fix bacon sandwiches and coffee, and we'd be off again, driving around the area, or catching a ferry to wherever we were filming. If the weather held, I would ride for umpteen hours until I'd landed a trick and Dave had got his shot. Afterwards, I would drive to the next location while Dave would check his footage in the back of the mobile home. It was quite a nice routine.

The van, unsurprisingly, was trashed. It was flimsy inside and there were quite a few parties in the back. They usually began once filming had finished. By the end of our adventure, it was barely watertight, the roof rack had been ripped off and all the blinds were wrecked. The kitchen units got smashed during one gathering; the beds were broken, the oven was knackered and the toilet, which had been converted into a makeshift bike shed, was in ruins.

The pinnacle of the filming came when I headed back to Dunvegan and rode around town, Dave shooting me as I cruised past the local police station. I couldn't believe I was making a living from my bicycle. I was hoping that, somewhere, PC Duncan Carmichael might pick up on the irony. I also rode a couple of lines over that red telephone box in the area, though in one landing the handlebars snapped, a jagged edge carving a big flap of skin from my palm. Later, we spent twelve days on the island of Raasay, just off the Isle of Skye, and built a mini freeride course on the hillside. An old iron mine was located there, so we also filmed in the foundations and over a railway track that led into the entrance. There was so much to play on.

Despite all that hard work, the returns weren't quite as exciting as we'd planned. When I first watched *Way Back Home*, I felt frustrated. Sure, there's a lot that we were proud of, especially the scenes on Edinburgh Castle and in Dunvegan. It's just that some parts didn't quite work out the way I'd hoped. My aspirations had been too high, and our work couldn't quite match them. We had fired all our energy into the tricks and the shooting process, yet I couldn't help but think back to those days of filming where I was unable to land all the stunts I'd planned, or sessions when the weather had turned.

That feeling didn't last too long, though, and there's a lot I like about *Way Back Home*. I'm happy with what we achieved; it just took me a while to come around. I also knew there would be plenty more videos to make and, with the help of Red Bull, lots more ideas to work on. In another stroke of luck, I got to hang out in the camper van until it fell apart at the seams.

I lived in that beast for another six months.

Scene Thirteen

(<u>INT.</u>) An indoor parking lot, New York City

Corrupt NYC detective Bobby Monday (Michael Shannon) is chasing down Wilee (Joseph Gordon-Levitt), a bicycle courier; Wilee is hiding with his bike among the cars. Bobby Monday is yelling at a uniformed police officer.

Wilee, on his bike, now played by stunt double Danny MacAskill, senses a chance to escape. He drops off a nearby ramp, lands on the roof of a car and pedals furiously. He then races over a series of bonnets as he rallies towards the exit.

Bobby Monday chases after him, but can't keep up. Wilee skids in front of a locked exit, turns and rides a series of rails, barriers and cars before escaping through a pair of closing gates, having made a 360 jump from a metal gangway ...

Premium Rush, 2012

INDUSTRIAL
REVOLUTIONS

Line across tops
of Trains

wire

Drop from rail
Manual Tih roof to Drop

180 Between Rails

Gap between Carriages

13. The Concrete Circus

As Dave and I were filming in Edinburgh one morning, a bus whizzed by. I can't remember where we were exactly, or what I was doing, but I won't forget the image in a hurry. On the side was a giant photo of my face. It was a shot taken from the S.1. Jobs advert I'd made a few months earlier. Now every bus in town carried a picture of me along the side, dressed in a suit, pulling a tailwhip on my Inspired bike. It freaked me out.

What the hell was going on?

Fame had never been my thing. I hadn't chased it, but if other riders saw what I was doing and liked it, well, that was enough for me. As for the commercial side of things, I used a hard-line psychological barometer. With every offer, I would think back to the younger version of myself, the one starting out in Macdonald Cycles. If he could look at whatever I was doing and think, Yeah, that's cool, then I was still in good shape. If not, I'd tell Tarek not to bother.

Crazy offers would come my way. During the making of *Way Back Home*, I was asked to work as a stunt double in the Hollywood action movie *Premium Rush*, which starred the former *Batman* actor Joseph Gordon-Levitt (spoiler alert: he played a homage to Robin). At first I wasn't that keen. The bicycle they wanted me to use wasn't a trials frame because I was due to be playing Gordon-Levitt's double, while *he* was playing a bicycle messenger being chased around New York City by a corrupt cop. Couriers tended to ride fixed-gear bicycles, a style I'd barely used but one that had become trendy – something I didn't want to be associated with – so I suggested a bunch of friends who were much more suited to the role than me. The producers weren't interested. When they later offered to have the script altered so I could use my Inspired, I eventually caved in. Anyway, after my scrapes with the Skye Police, I figured I could slip into character quite easily, and so I flew to New York, where the movie was underway.

I had zero experience of film sets. Luckily, Joseph Gordon-Levitt was hardly a diva. In fact, he was a genuinely sound dude. The stunts were also a fair bit easier than flipping myself off castle battlements. I had to race across parked cars and plastic traffic barriers before 360ing off a ledge. It seemed super-simple compared to stressing over the parts at Raasay and Skye.

I've been wary of working for TV because the riding is portrayed in a different style. During the making of *Inspired Bicycles* and *Way Back Home*, Dave and me had focused on style and tricks rather than drama. In TV documentaries the stereotypical cycling image is a biker flying through the sky; TV rarely captures a sense of just how challenging or difficult street trials riding is.

So when Channel 4 approached me in 2011 with the idea of appearing in a show called *Concrete Circus*, I wasn't that fussed. But once I'd spoken to producer and director Mike Christie, I changed my mind. *Concrete Circus* promised to be a little bit different, the idea being that it featured four riders, each of them makers of their own internet virals. Among Mike's roll-call of contributors were freestyle skateboarder Kilian Martin and pro flatland BMXer Keelan Phillips. He'd also convinced parkour duo Blue and Phil Doyle from London team Storm Freerun to work on the project. Meanwhile, creative control would rest with the riders and those making the film rather than Channel 4. Basically, I was being asked to make my own video, funded by a TV company's budget, and that sounded like a lot of fun.

When I told Mike that I was up for it, my first thought was to team up with Dave Sowerby again. We had put some great stuff together in the past. There was one downside, however. During the making of *Way Back Home*, I had burned Dave out – big style. The process had been a bit of a struggle for the pair of us and, while Dave was incredibly patient throughout, the project was knackering. I don't know exactly how many days we spent out on the road, but he was with me for every second as we drove up and down the country, filming and riding. Dave was also wary of getting involved with a mainstream TV company.

That's when I thought of the former Mountain Bike World Cup rider Stu Thomson. He was a good friend, and I knew him to be a great director, though he was just beginning his career. After an ankle injury had put him out of the downhill scene for good, he started a company called MTB Cut. This was at a time when the internet was only just kicking off, but Stu had enjoyed a little success by making same-day video reports of the Mountain Bike World Cup. He would upload them as soon as they had been edited, which was quite ahead of the game in racing terms. Stu seemed really switched on business-wise. He was also very creative. He had a director's eye, and it later became his style to make cinematic videos that were quite epic in vibe.

I figured shooting with him might be fun. Stu was up for it, too. Our only problem was the deadline. Because the pair of us had hectic schedules, we initially struggled to find time in our diaries even to begin. By the time we'd finally got together, everybody else had finished their respective projects, so Kilian Martin visited Skye to hang out. That was surreal. I'd only ever seen him in virals before. While I'd been in New York making *Premium Rush*, my friend Nash showed me one of his videos and it had blown me away. Kilian was amazing; his flow was so smooth and he seemed so graceful on a skateboard. He was able to mix old-school, flatland riding with big new-school tricks. He was operating within his own scene.

Meeting him put the pressure on. With our deadline looming, Stu and me still hadn't even found a location. I was all out of ideas, because in my head I'd checked out pretty much all of Scotland, having scouted the country for several months during the making of *Way Back Home*. Nothing anyone suggested seemed novel or exciting.

'Where the heck are we going to go, Stu?' I grumbled. 'There aren't many places in Scotland I've not been to . . .'

Stu decided to switch things up. He got the idea into his head that we should start in an abandoned location, somewhere with character, derelict and off the beaten track. We spent hours scouring Google Images for spaces until, one rainy afternoon, it came to us: a picture of Dunaskin Ironworks, an old site that had lain abandoned since 1988. In the photos, Dunaskin looked great. Its exterior had been bookended by two giant chimneys, façades comprising faded brickwork and two rusting gates. There were crumbling walls to jump over, rail tracks to gap and abandoned trains to climb on.

On closer inspection, it turned out to be the perfect place for a video. Everything was rusting – the stairs, the railings and the abandoned trains. Dunaskin had also been an old power station, and so there were six acres of land for us to play in. The map was covered in ruined buildings, old kilns which had been used to smelt iron and a derelict railway yard with disused train tracks and several steam locomotives.

Because the work was concentrated in such a small area, we were able to tie a loose story together. The disused buildings gave us a sense of abandonment. We had a theme, and milked that place for all it was worth. We finished the shoot in six solid days and named our piece *Industrial Revolutions* as a nod to our location.

Once I've finished filming a video, there's usually an intense discussion about the soundtrack, based on my mental longlist of bands and songs. But in the case of *Industrial Revolutions* everything was figured out back to front. Stu had a contact at the record label Universal. Probably because our project was going to be screened on terrestrial telly, he had no problem securing a licensing deal, and we were sent some tracks to play with.

One CD was 'The Wolves', a single by the English singer-songwriter Ben Howard, and the music seemed to fit with everything we were attempting. Before we'd even finished, I knew it was the perfect match and, weirdly, having it in mind helped the filming. Stu would open the doors of his van and cue up the track. As I rode over train carriages, or gapped railings, he would play 'The Wolves' at full blast. Often I would time my run to coincide with a lyrical cue or a guitar riff and we captured some cool one-off tricks: for example, I managed to ride across a tightrope-style cable that had been suspended between two disused train carriages.

It was those lines that grabbed the public's imagination. After the show was released in August 2011, motorbike racer Guy Martin raved about it on Twitter. Meanwhile, folk were buzzing about the *Concrete Circus* documentary, which had featured some amazing parts from Kilian, Storm Freerun and Keelan. I was pretty pleased with it. It's one of my favourite films so far, but the TV exposure hadn't excited me at all. Any extra publicity was another means to an end, especially if it raised my chances of making a few more films. Besides, it wasn't as if I craved a boost in profile. My face was on the side of just about every bus in Edinburgh, and that was enough to make me squirm.

Bad news followed good.

My left leg was a mess and I couldn't figure out what was up with it. Throughout much of *Industrial Revolutions*, I could barely walk properly, and the joints in my knee kept seizing up. For six days, I dragged myself about, necking painkillers, just so I could make it through the filming.

Once I'd been given a chance to rest up, I put the injury to one side; the intensity seemed to fade. That was a relief because I was down to feature in a big mountain-bike production called *Strength in Numbers* in Vancouver with some amazing riders, including Gee Atherton, Wade Simmons and Anthony Messere. Having explored the Scottish countryside for the best part of eight months, I was eager to film in a more urban setting. The movie was being made by Anthill Films, one of the scene's best film-makers; each person involved with *Strength in Numbers* had been given a stand-alone section, which was a big deal. Being in that kind of video took me out of YouTube and validated my place in the mountain-bike world even more. I was shoulder to shoulder with some of the world's best – and in a showcase movie.

Excitement quickly turned to frustration. I'd put aside eight weeks to work in Canada, and after a fortnight of location scouting I still felt physically restricted. My leg was weak. I couldn't figure out why and, when I tried to tyre-tap off a log in Stanley Park, a beautiful spot in Vancouver city centre, I bailed off the bike, falling awkwardly. As I landed, my left foot slipped in a pile of goose crap, which caused my left knee to buckle beneath me. I could feel the muscles tearing and pulling in and around my knee, wrenching at my meniscus. I was in a lot of pain, unable to walk or cycle, and a six-week period of recovery in Vancouver couldn't heal the injury. Even more frustrating was the fact that I had injured myself thirty minutes into a six-week project. *Man alive.*

After a productive year, I was out of the game again. There were so many opportunities ahead of me, chances to investigate different locations and try new tricks, yet here I was locked into a routine where injury seemed to follow every video. That hacked me off, especially as Red Bull was keen for me to make another viral.

My patience was being severely tested . . .

Scene Fourteen

(<u>INT.</u>) The Glasgow Transport Museum

Danny rides his bike across the top of a decommissioned army tank. He's surrounded by life-size 'toy soldiers' — friends dressed in military fatigues; their costumes have been painted a shade of green.

Gliding along the gun barrel, Danny reaches the end. He leans forward, lifts his back wheel and pulls a 360-degree footjam, but . . . Ouch! Danny's front tyre slips. His bike falls at an awkward angle. In the crash, he topples to the floor, landing flat on his back. Three toy soldiers gather round. They're checking his motionless body. Off camera, there is a shout.

Danny has blacked out . . .

Imaginate, Closing Credits, 2013

Ambulance

14. Wrecked

I've got a relatively modest checklist of broken bones and shredded tendons . . .

- *Left foot, broken (three times)*
- *Right foot, torn ligaments (twice)*
- *Left meniscus, torn*
- *Index finger, dislocated*
- *Right wrist, broken*
- *Right arm, an operation to clean out a gouged wound*
- *Lower back, operation*
- *Left collarbone, broken (three times)*

Compared to many extreme athletes, I've been lucky. I think it's because I don't require high speeds for success like a top-level moto-cross freestyler or downhill racer. There, the forces involved in a collision are much bigger – and a lot more dangerous. Our bodies are all the same, and falling off a trials bike can still be pretty risky, but if I was regularly coming off a race bicycle at full pelt, I'd have broken a few more bones and lost a lot more skin by now.

14. Me on Inspired bike, Edinburgh, 2009.

15. Filming end sequence for *Imaginate*, Kelvin Hall, Glasgow, March 2013.

16. Filming end sequence for *Imaginate*, Kelvin Hall, Glasgow, March 2013.

17. *From right to left*: Nash Mason, Stu Thomson, Dave Mackison, Robbie Meade, reviewing footage for *Imaginate*, March 2013.

18. Back flip off a sketchy
girder in Epecuén, Argentina,
March 2014.

19. Me inside Mataredo
Building, Epecuén,
Argentina, March 2014.

20. *From right to left*: Lec Park flying the drone, Scott Marshal and Stu Thomson standing on the top of Cullin Ridge, Isle of Skye, June 2014.

21. The Dream Team, *from right to left*: Donnie Macphie, Paul Smail, Lec Park, Alan Blyth, Stu Thomson, me, John, Chris Prescott, Scott Marshal, Paul Diffley, Matt Barratt, Andy McCandlish on Glen Brittle beach, Isle of Skye, June 2014.

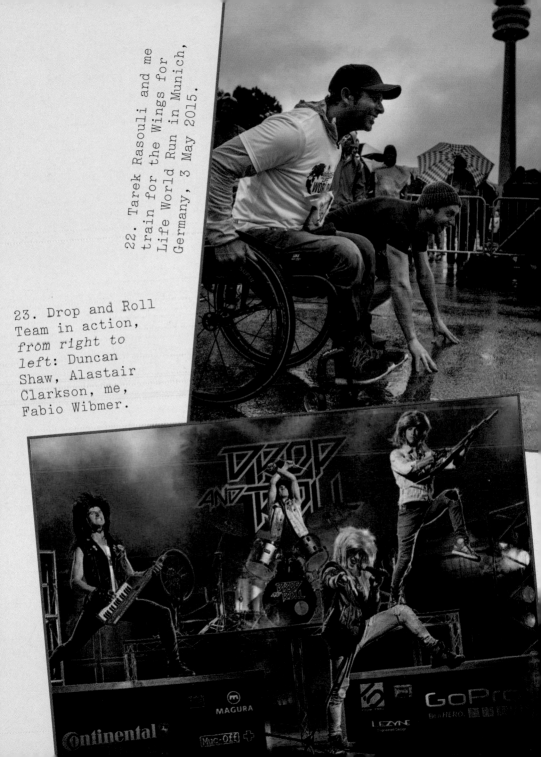

22. Tarek Rasouli and me train for the Wings for Life World Run in Munich, Germany, 3 May 2015.

23. Drop and Roll Team in action, *from right to left*: Duncan Shaw, Alastair Clarkson, me, Fabio Wibmer.

24. Me back-flipping between three-storey high-school buildings, filming for GoPro film *Cascadia*, Las Palmas, Gran Canaria, October 2015.

25. Me looking out from boat
over the Firth of Forth to
the Forth Railway Bridge,
near Edinburgh, while filming
Way Back Home, September 2010.

I've always considered injury to be an occupational hazard, in the same way that a fireman might hurt himself while putting out a blaze. But not everyone sees it that way. People have criticized me, and other athletes, who operate in action sports for taking risks. Except everything's relative: I've never taken on a stunt that I've thought might kill me; everything I do has to be within my capabilities.

I reckon it's the same with all extreme-sports folk. Take free climbers like Alex Honnold. Whenever he's scaled a cliff face, rope-free, Alex has planned it all out in advance. He'll scale the route with ropes beforehand. In the same way that I've used mats to prepare for some of my jumps, he'll assess his climb first, which allows him to remain calm and confident while he's up there. Most of the time, Alex probably operates at a level that's comfortable for him, even though it might look terrifying to everyone else, especially when he's dangling from an overhanging cliff face hundreds of metres up with only his fingertips to hold him in place.

People are happy to criticize athletes like Alex, or me, for doing a dangerous sport in which we're experienced, yet they'll race along a country road in the pouring rain, or go on a skiing holiday, and think nothing of it. And why would they? They're not doing anything that dangerous – in theory. The reality is different, though. There are other people around, and that's what puts them at risk. There are car crashes all the time; skiers can injure other skiers, often when one of them is riding perfectly well on their own. I'm only risking myself. I'm not putting anyone else in harm's way.

In the meantime, I've accepted that injury is something I'll have to live with. That doesn't make it any easier to handle whenever it comes along, though. I get grumpy. I can moan a lot. But I've learned there are ways to avoid the bad moods. Having a project in mind can help, and I'll usually focus on that. I'll think of new stunts. I'll search out different locations and soundtracks. Most of the time, though, I have to accept the diagnosis and focus on my recovery. I'll tell myself that I'm broken and that I need to 'rest'. *Just do what you have to do to get back on the bike* . . . It becomes a bit of a boring mantra, but it works.

When I'm fully fit and making a video, like I was during the shooting of *Inspired Bicycles,* I always savour the feeling of being in one piece, usually when I step into the shower in the morning. I don't know whether that's because I've just woken up and my brain's beginning to click into gear, or if I'm naturally doing a lot of thinking about riding and the day ahead, but I appreciate the comfortable movement. There's no pain, no broken bones; no slings or plaster casts. Everything's fully functional, and it feels great.

Sometimes, being fit can seem like a novelty. I think I've been away from the bike for three out of the last five years with one injury or another. But that's when I focus on dreaming up my next video or sketching out a line. It gives me something to feel positive about. I can explore, too. When I broke my collarbone during the making of *Way Back Home,* I spent a lot of time in my friend's car. I drove around Scotland, searching for cool locations. I found disused buildings next to lochs and obstacles around Edinburgh. With each discovery, I could see the tricks and feel the sensations in my mind.

Mentally, at least, my riding seemed to improve, too – even though I hadn't been able to put my feet on the pedals. I *visualized* landing the tricks. The filming I was planning became more ambitious. My ideas became bolder and, with every week, I progressed a little bit more – but only in my mind. I've since learned that this form of thinking is a common psychological ploy used by injured sports stars. There's even theorizing that suggests it's possible for someone to build strength and skill when they've been unable to train. They mentally envisage development and improvement, and their body reacts accordingly.

Apparently, the British Olympic javelin thrower Steve Backley used a similar technique, and with amazing results. Just fourteen weeks before the 1996 Olympic Games in Atlanta, he was sidelined with a ruptured Achilles tendon. In that time, Backley visualized what he would do once he was fully fit. He imagined himself competing – throw after throw after throw. He even pictured the stadiums he would be working in. All of them were packed with crowds. By the time of his recovery, which happened just in time for him to appear at Atlanta, he reckons he'd visualized hundreds and hundreds of hurled javelins. All of them reached their target. Despite the fact that he hadn't done any of the physical preparation during the run-up to competition – the throwing, jumping or sprinting aspects of his training – he won a silver medal.

I'd been doing the same thing, though with slightly different results. My mind might have been sharper once I'd regained full fitness, and the tricks in my head were a lot more ambitious, but my body had other ideas to begin with. On my first ride after recovering from that broken collarbone, as I began shooting *Way Back Home*, I could barely do a manual, and it was quite a shock. That didn't last long; everything soon clicked into place. After a few weeks I felt like I was approaching my form of 2009, but there was still plenty of hard graft involved. At first, it was frustrating. I got annoyed that I was unable to physically execute the ideas that I'd planned out in my mind. Then I learned to savour the sensation of being fully fit again. It got my head straight; my riding came together. That was a real privilege, as I've learned from the people around me.

My checklist could be a hell of a lot worse.

Strength in Numbers was blown. Slipping in goose crap had aggravated my back and knee, and I was in a lot of pain. Whenever I moved, it was as if someone was grabbing the tendons in the back of my leg with a pair of pliers and, after scans at the DISC Sports & Spine Center in Marina del Rey, California, courtesy of Red Bull, my issue was diagnosed: a bone spur, a pinched nerve and congenital spinal stenosis. If that wasn't enough, there was also a partially ruptured disc to deal with, which had been damaged a year or so earlier while I'd been making the S.1. Jobs advert.

I distinctly remember doing it, too. I'd 360'd down a

twelve-foot drop several times, and on the last attempt I felt my back tweak. As I recovered from the collarbone injuries, the rupture became progressively worse, especially once my core strength had been wiped out. During that time, all the muscles in my lower back had been weakened; the support for my disc was diminished. Now it was ripped open and, with every severe movement, acidic fluid was being squirted from the tear and on to my nerve. I was in a lot of pain. We decided I should have an operation to sort out the issue.

DISC had a serious reputation, having treated a long list of international athletes and Hollywood legends. Red Bull stars such as Ian Walsh (big-wave surfing), Mike Day (BMX) and the 100-metre-hurdles Olympic finalist Lolo Jones had passed through the clinic. On the walls were framed thank-you notes from the likes of Sylvester Stallone, Jennifer Lawrence and, weirdly, the Teenage Ninja Mutant Turtles. I was to be treated by the neurological spine surgeon Dr Robert Bray. Meanwhile, my rehab was to be under the supervision of 'Hall of Fame strength and conditioning coach' Dr E. J. 'Doc' Kreis.

Doc was a character. Back in the day, he had been heavily involved with treating injured American footballers, mostly athletes from the University of Central Los Angeles. Later, I was introduced to my physio, Dr Joe Horrigan, who had worked out of the Gold Gym body-building scene located on Venice Beach, California. Famously, Gold had produced Arnold Schwarzenegger, among others, but Dr Horrigan wasn't interested in reliving any of *his* past successes. As soon as I'd mentioned my surname, he peered up from his clipboard with a quizzical look.

'MacAskill from Scotland?' he said. 'Are you familiar with the legend of Angus MacAskill?'

When I confirmed that, yes, I was, and he was a relative, Dr Horrigan was delighted. He bombarded me with questions. God knows how he had learned about Angus, but he became obsessed with my stories about Dad's museum and my ancestor's crazy life story.

Despite the high spirits at DISC, it wasn't long before I was out cold, a surgical knife cutting into my back. The operation to fix my injury clearly took place at a busy time of year because, when I came round, still groggy from the anaesthetic, I could see a couple of people in the recovery room, including moto-cross freestyle legend Robbie Maddison. (Maybe DISC had offered Red Bull a two-for-one deal.)

I'd never met Robbie before, but I was a fan of his riding. He's a modern-day Evel Knievel and some of the stunts he's done have been *insane*. During one film he flew 278 feet across the Corinth Canal in Greece on his motorcycle, and he built a jump that took him across the length of an American football field in another. So, after a few moments of 'Should I, shouldn't I?', and still feeling woozy from morphine, I wobbled over.

'Hey, Robbie,' I said. 'How's it going?'

Robbie looked up, bleary-eyed. Somehow, through the anaesthetic, there was a flash of recognition. (Or maybe he was good at pretending.) We got to talking – well, as best you can when you're doped up to the eyeballs on painkillers – and that's when he told me he'd caught a few of my online films. We chatted about his plans and our injuries; we talked through some film ideas, too. It was a good way to take my mind off surgery. I'd almost forgotten that my arse was hanging out the back of a surgical gown.

Once the stitches in my back had been taken out, Doc started roughing me up in rehab. God, it was hard. I wasn't one for stepping into a gym, and I hadn't stretched my muscles properly since PE at school. Doc had his own ideas and, most mornings, I was on the floor, working my body this way and that. Under the watchful gaze of several DISC specialists, my recovery period operated to a time-table more extreme than anything I'd been used to before. I was up at six every morning for a tortuous shift of stretch-ing, cardio exercise and weight training that had me sweating for three hours. It was full on.

The plan was twofold. I was to get back into shape so I could ride again, but the strength and conditioning training would also make me tougher, and more flexible, than ever before. It was going to be a long process. The experts esti-mated it would take eleven months in total before I could cut about on a bike again. Luckily, I had a project in mind, something to take my focus away from the hard slog – an idea that would later grab my attention for the best part of a year.

Initially, I'd decided that I wanted a broad working brief for my next film, as wide as anyone could have hoped for. There was no real jumping-off point so I gave myself free rein, allowing my mind to wander and come up with as many new tricks and set-ups as possible (some of which may or may not have involved an elephant, a ramp and a piece of twine). I was up for planning the video of my dreams and would spend hours fantasizing about what I could do on my bike and where, scribbling down ideas in a notepad as fast as I came up with them.

By the end of my time at DISC, I was fired up. I had a plan to move forward. Dreaming of a new project had been a good move. It gave me the perfect distraction during what could have been a miserable spell away from the bike. Instead, I had something to focus on as I made my way through the recovery process. And I didn't moan once.

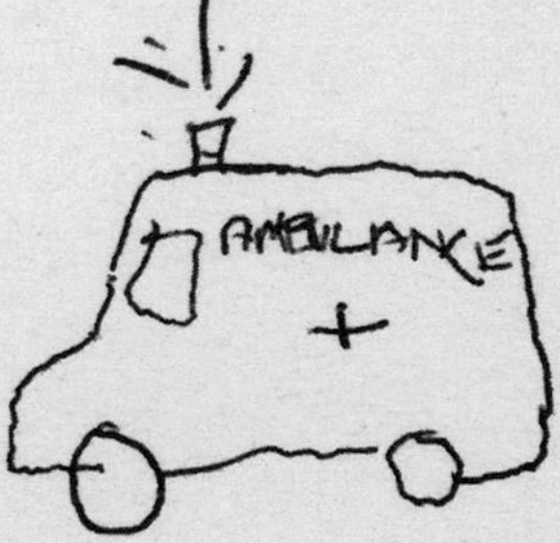
AMBULANCE

Scene Fifteen

<u>FADE IN</u>

(<u>INT.</u>) The Glasgow Transport Museum

Danny is stressed. He's riding around the
Transport Museum, now a playground of obstacles
and jumps, with his headphones on. The camera
crew, including director Stu Thomson, wait
patiently. In the distance is Danny's next
challenge: a ramp made from four giant-sized
playing cards. At the front is a five of
diamonds.

STU: We're trying to film a line that has become
Danny's nemesis. This is the fifth day we've
tried. Every time, it's just not happened and
it's built up to be something in his head . . .

Danny circles the ramp, but he can't commit to
jumping. He rides up the transition and rolls
off. Stu taps his forehead in frustration.

STU: It's a complete mental game. It's not even
physical any more — can he, or can't he, do the
trick? It's: Can he get past what's going on in
his head?

MacAskill's Imaginate, Episode 5, 2013

15. No Limits

Imaginate was to be a video without limitations.

Inspired Bicycles had been about street riding; *Way Back Home* and *Industrial Revolutions* had been made in epic outdoor locations, but I was fed up with waiting for the Scottish sun to come out from behind the clouds. It rarely did, so the logical step was to take my filming into a studio, where I could build whatever I wanted. I had a blank canvas, so I listed all the stunts I wanted to capture, and nothing was out of bounds . . .

— *Loop the loop!*
— *Riding over a rainbow*
— *A trampoline bounce*
— *The Sheep Chariot*
— *A tunnel slide (with a sneaky costume change halfway down)*

Our only issue was finding a space big enough to house all the props and ramps I needed if I was to make a spectacular indoor trials course. Somebody suggested moving into a warehouse next to the Olympic Park in east London, but I had the feeling it would be better for me, both psychologically and physically, if we stayed in Glasgow. My back was still healing, and my head wasn't in a good place. I didn't have enough riding in me either. I'd been off the bike all summer and hadn't done any decent filming since *Industrial Revolutions*. Whenever my body felt good, my mind felt good; I knew I could withstand a succession of crashes, and so the riding benefited. My confidence was usually high in those times, too, as was my ambition, which was what drove the ideas. But in the run-up to *Imaginate* I was in a different headspace. I was coming up with tricks, but I wasn't sure whether I'd be physically capable of seeing them through.

At first I was reluctant to put final concepts down on paper. I couldn't commit. Luckily, I wasn't feeling any pressure from outside forces such as Red Bull, or Stu, who was returning as my director. OK, so there wasn't a rush to get anything finished, but I still felt stressed, and all the heat was coming from me. I wanted to make the most of this opportunity and I needed to concentrate, but because my back wasn't right, my riding wasn't where I needed it to be and so the process felt a bit strange. I also felt nervous, and my rehabilitation wasn't helping. The doctors, and my Red Bull trainer, Darren Roberts, had assured me that my ruptured disc was healing and that I would be fine, but it didn't feel like it.

I needed to get back on the bike to clear my mind, to visualize properly, but physically I was still some way short of being able to do anything overly ambitious. Fortunately, we managed to find a location much closer to home in which we could think about building a set. I'd heard the Glasgow Transport Museum in Kelvin Hall was lying empty. The owners had moved into a new building, somewhere on the bonny banks of the River Clyde and, unbelievably, when we contacted them, they said I could have it for free. All I had to do was to finalize the tricks and come up with a theme.

The old Transport Museum was a cavernous space and, for some reason, the owners had left behind a life-size replica train platform, complete with rails. The 'station' even had a tiny waiting room, and an old Scotrail engine had been parked alongside. As soon as I walked in, I had the idea we should stick a Dunvegan sign to the side as a nod to home. (By the way, I wouldn't waste your time asking for a train ticket to Dunvegan – we haven't got a station.)

That's when the concept hit me. Flicking through a notepad, I'd been struck by how childlike my visualizations could be. Leonardo-style diagrams didn't feature in my portfolio. Most of my designs had been scrawled down in pen and involved stick men, plus some arrows and weird notes. *And my handwriting was terrible – like a kid's!* And that's when I thought, What if I regressed? When I was a wee lad, I didn't own a miniature toy motorbike. Instead, I would imagine my fork or my pencil was a racer or a BMX. I'd jump around other everyday objects as if they were huge ramps or gaps.

Hang on, I thought. What if the set was a child's bedroom and we built everything like an episode of *The Borrowers*? Me on my bike, shrunk down, riding over a floor full of stuff. Like a toy come to life! We already have a train set, after all . . .

From there, the idea grew arms and legs. Anything that could conceivably be found in a boy's bedroom, like a space-ship or a plastic gun, could be built, giant-sized, as a surface for me to ride over. Red Bull loved the concept and, from there, we had our base to bring in other props, so for three months we designed giant children's building blocks, twelve-foot-long colouring pencils, toy soldiers (my nephew Thomas and a couple of friends dressed up), *Dandy* annuals and a huge deck of playing cards; there was even a giant Red Bull air bag to practise on. A lot of the props were built by George and John from Vision Ramps; pencils were carved from telegraph poles by my friend Davey and brought into Kelvin Hall, where we could set them out on the floor. Meanwhile, a fake wall, a carpet and a skirting board (which was eleven feet high) had been put together. Nothing was off limits. When somebody built a super-sized game of Twister and I was able to ride around on the spinner, nobody batted an eyelid.

Somewhere, in the middle of our crazy playground, I'd wanted a tank. The idea had been fixed in my head for months so, along with Stu, we set about borrowing a Second World War armoured vehicle from a local collector in Dum-fries. It was a beast. A lorry delivered it to the end of the road and a bunch of folk outside stopped in their tracks and gawped – they must have thought we were being invaded. Exhaust fumes poured from the top as it chuntered outside

Kelvin Hall and, when I saw the tank sliding across the back of the room, its gun barrel looming into view, I was stoked.

The tank was cool, but not as cool as the F1 car that Red Bull Racing had kindly – or somewhat bravely – loaned to us for filming: all four and a half million quid of it. The body sparkled and gleamed as it was unveiled from underneath a dustsheet. I couldn't believe they had brought it in. Nor could the delivery guy who had been tasked with looking after its well-being. A fussy fellow who was clearly questioning the sanity of loaning such an expensive piece of kit to a dude on a mountain bike, he spent at least ten minutes telling us what we could and couldn't do around the car. (Clue: there were a lot more 'couldn't's than 'could's.) Red Bull had also charged a guard to tag along and keep watch, just in case one of us had the crazy brainwave of taking it around Glasgow for a quick spin.

Once our briefing had been completed, the delivery man offered to give the paintwork a final polish and pulled a can from the cockpit, squirting a dollop of liquid on the rear wing.

Hmm, I thought. That's got to be some fancy polish, it's come out all silver . . .

As a cloth was used to massage the blob of metallic-looking goo across the car's exterior, it became obvious that some terrible cock-up had taken place. The polish wasn't polish at all but spray paint – an application that had probably been used for the alloy wheels of the trailer that the car had been delivered on. Somebody had left a can of the stuff in the cockpit and Red Bull's courier was now smearing it across the body. As the realization sunk in, a look of panic flashed across his face. We all knew that recoating a multimillion-quid motor was going to cost a fortune. Anything I was intending to do on it seemed like small change now.

Throughout the making of *Imaginate*, I was a nightmare to work with. Despite my rehab, I was still experiencing a lot of back pain. Some days were good; a lot of them bad. I tried to get into the swing of things by riding around town with Martyn Ashton, and I later cut about Glasgow with the Olympic flame as part of the build-up to London 2012, which was a buzz. But even though I could ride, I was in pain, and once we got to working I experienced a series of highs and lows. Sometimes I found it almost impossible to get out of bed.

Once I'd started riding properly, and the cameras were rolling, I became a bit of a slave driver. I was super-focused on doing the lines to the best of my ability – I had come up with them, after all. But I was also operating to a heavy, physical schedule. Most mornings were spent in the gym, where I worked on rehab exercises, usually from seven thirty. The crew would arrive in the studio at around nine, and we would start shooting a stunt. The aim was always to get one in the bag before lunchtime. If that happened, we would go to the little café around the corner to celebrate, though it rarely worked out that way. Often we would film until ten o'clock at night without leaving Kelvin Hall.

Because of my injury, and a diminished confidence, tricks that should have been completed in a day took four. It was hard going for everybody.

There was also an elephant in the room: our banger, a twenty-foot-tall, brightly coloured loop-the-loop. Back in the day, loads of kids had played with a Hot Wheels track in their bedrooms, and all of them came with a loop-the-loop. I'd always wanted to ride one, and my plan had been to back-flip out of a giant air vent that had been constructed into our fake wall. I would then drop down on to a 'ramp' – a copy of a *Dandy* annual that was *huge* – building up enough speed to curve up our oversized track, upside down.

My only issue was riding the thing. I had never done a loop before and, once I'd suggested the idea, I scoured the internet, looking for riders who had captured one on video. Whenever I saw anyone attempting it, professional or amateur, on any contraption, it usually ended in tears. There were some disgusting crashes. I watched as people flew out of the side halfway round, or riders went in too fast, arcing up and out of the top. Even watching the footage was disorientating. With my injury thrown into the mix, the challenge felt overwhelming.

One day, I'm going to have to hit that thing, I'd think, staring at the construction in the studio as production began.

In Stu's head, that stunt was one component within a complicated sequence, which he hoped would become the video's banger. After I'd emerged from the loop in one piece, I was faced with a small wedge. I had to use that as a kicker to front-flip over the F1 car that had been positioned underneath, complete with silver streak marks. It was tough, but I knew the line was going to be worth it – it would look great with Stu's camerawork and editing. Still, every trick was a trying physical test, even under the best of circumstances. With injury playing on my mind, the stress levels were extra high.

Thankfully, when I flipped out of the air vent for the first time and landed on the *Dandy*, my back held strong. It was only once I'd got to the bottom that I found trouble. I felt a little dizzy, nauseous. At first I blamed my spinning head and churning stomach on a lack of breakfast; I hadn't eaten properly. But as the day wore on, I became progressively worse, until I had to lie down. I felt like puking, and everything was whirling around. The sensation wasn't too dissimilar to being drunk. As a precaution, I was packed off to hospital for a CT scan, where I was diagnosed with labyrinthitis, a condition that affects the inner ear and balance. I was out of the shoot for another three weeks.

The recovery was slow. For the first week I had a serious case of the whirlies. Nausea rocked me for days. During the second week I was able to get back on the bike again, though I was still very dizzy, but it really helped my mood, and once I was riding regularly during week three, I realized the break had done me good. We had been filming *Imaginate* for five weeks. At times, the work had felt a little like

Groundhog Day. I would ride indoors for hours, going home to bed so I could psych myself into doing it all over again. All my friends working on the project were feeling a lot of pressure, but it seemed to hit me the hardest. Mentally, I was drained because I hadn't been smashing out the riding like I was used to.

With rest, I was stronger and, despite the psychological hurdles and hitches, riding the loop was extremely fun. I could back-flip out of the air vent with ease, freewheeling down the *Dandy* and into the curve. Having watched all those YouTube clips – some good, plenty bad – I knew I'd have to maintain a steady line to prevent myself from going out and coming off at a hellish angle. I gripped my handlebars steady, keeping my arms and legs firm. I had enough momentum to ride around the loop in one swift movement. Before I knew it, I was firing out of the other end like a bullet.

I was stoked. That one line had played out in the back of my mind every day for a month. For a week I would use the loop as a morning warm-up, it was that much fun. After physio, I would show up at the Transport Museum, get on the bike and drop out of the air vent. For half an hour, I'd ride it over and over – it was a little play before the real work began.

We worked for sixty days, with some heavy crashes, though the only serious fall arrived when I slipped off the tank's gun barrel. I had cruised to the end, pulling my back wheel up and kicking into a 360 footjam tailwhip. But as the frame spun, I lost the grip in my front tyre and was thrown off. The bike went one way, my body the other, and from there I bounced hard on the steel gun, falling eight feet to the concrete floor. Nothing could stop me from landing directly on my back and, as I tried to get up, a stabbing pain pinned me to the deck; the room began to spin. I couldn't breathe, because the impact had knocked all the air from my lungs. My muscles trembled, and I felt nothing. I blacked out.

It was probably only seconds before I came round. My vision quickly readjusted to the scenes above me: worried, staring faces; my friends dressed as Second World War soldiers, the shadow of a giant tank. I gulped in a breath.

'Wow,' I moaned. 'This is the weirdest dream . . .'

I checked myself over. Luckily, there was no real lasting pain in my lower back; everything seemed fine and, mentally, the fall had toughened me up. Knowing I could take a serious knock and not have it sideline me was reassuring, though there were other psychological glitches during the making of *Imaginate*. Like an author struggling with writer's block, I could sometimes find myself hung up on a line or a jump. Usually, it was a stunt I could have ordinarily landed with my eyes shut, but it became insurmountable. For example, for this video I wanted to flair on a ramp comprising four giant 'playing cards' – ply sheets designed to look like a two of clubs and the five of diamonds. It should have been fairly straightforward because I'd done plenty of flairs before and the technique wasn't too dissimilar to the one I'd filmed during the making of *Inspired Bicycles*: I had to ride up and pop out of the top, spinning my body in the air before landing on to the playing cards again.

What made the *Imaginate* flair so difficult was the fact that our set-up was built from a series of overlapping, flat panels, which made for a bumpy transition. We wasted four days trying to capture the shot with no real luck, and the five of diamonds became a mental block. I could not get the technique right. I would ride to the lip of the card and pull away; I circled the line for ages. My biggest problem was that I kept carving too far, which caused me to miss my landing at the end. Forget the spiky fence in *Inspired Bicycles* – this was a whole other level of frustration.

I don't have any phobias, but the five of diamonds seemed to bring out a weird reaction in me. Every time I saw it, I felt angry. I tried everything to flick the switch, to fool my brain into riding the line correctly, but nothing seemed to work. At times, Stu would send me off to ride the loop for therapy. He knew it would cheer me up. On other days, I'd shut myself away with my phone and some tunes. I hoped that would break my spiral of negativity.

At five o'clock on the final day of shooting I found myself staring down the barrel of that five of diamonds again. Maybe it was because the studio was being packed down. Maybe it was because we were, quite literally, into the final moments of studio time but, somehow, I was able to shift my focus. A trigger in my head told me to '*GO!*', and I rode at the ramp, firing across the slope and taking off at the top. As I went up, I brought the bike around myself in a flair, landing on the two of clubs and rolling away.

I could hear shouting. George leapt on top of me; the camera crew were going nuts. However, I didn't want to celebrate, I just wanted to check the shot to make sure I had got it dialled. I wasn't that excited. In fact, I was still raging. That five of diamonds had messed with my mind. I was more relieved that I'd ended a minor mental meltdown, not to mention a week of sleepless nights, stressing over a trick that had become my nemesis. I never wanted to look at a pack of playing cards again.

Scene Sixteen

(<u>EXT.</u>) A pub garden, somewhere in West
Yorkshire

Danny is dressed in road-biking gear: red Lycra
shorts, matching Lycra top and a Red Bull-branded
helmet. He's riding a carbon-framed Colnago
C59 disc.

A pub bench is resting upright on its shortest
side. Danny rides to the flat bench top at speed,
hopping into it so his weight knocks the legs
into their correct position, leaving him
balancing on top.

He gives the camera a thumbs-up, but the frame
wobbles underneath him. He seems uncomfortable
on an unfamiliar bike . . .

                    Road Bike Party 2, 2013

Ride over Bridge

Manchester Loop
↳ On Road Bike?

↑
Wooden Run up

Tip Bench

16. The Closest Shaves

I don't suffer from sleepless nights about what could happen while riding, and I rarely think about worst-case scenarios. But I'm a realist. I work with people who have lived through life-changing injuries.

Take my manager, Tarek Rasouli. As a pro, he used to be a big player in the mountain-bike and freeride world, a representative for Race Face/Rocky Mountain and Red Bull, but when he broke his spine in 2002 on a large step-down in Canada, it left him in a wheelchair. It may have ended his bike career, but it didn't change his determination and character – not in the slightest. Tarek later set up his management operation Rasoulution and took on some top athletes. Thanks to him, a lot of mountain bikers have been able to make a decent living from the scene.

In the world of action sports, serious injuries are not uncommon. Tarek's spinal injury sent a ripple though the freeride community, and a few years later the BMX world was hit with the news that legendary dirt jump BMXer

Stephen Murray had become paralysed after a crash. Though I did not know Stephen, people around me later suffered similar tragedies. In 2013, my friend Michael Bonney was involved in a nasty crash and severed his spinal cord. He became a C3 tetraplegic. Another friend of mine, Tommy Wilkinson, did the same thing and lost the use of an arm. In a blog on dirtmountainbike.com he wrote, 'I'd damaged the spinal cord between c3-c7, dislocated c6, fractured my fairly dense skull, broken my collarbone and torn three nerves of the brachial plexus straight out my spinal cord.' Things like this really make you take a step back and think . . .

In September that same year, Martyn Ashton – probably my main influence growing up, all-round trials hero and now friend – had a serious fall at the Animal WD40 Action Sports Tour, fracturing the t9 and t10 vertebrae in his spine. He's been confined to a wheelchair ever since. The performance was taking place at the Silverstone MotoGP and, like a lot of serious bike accidents, nothing seemed out of the ordinary on the day. Martyn was doing a familiar routine, one he'd gone through at shows hundreds and hundreds of times, most probably, but one trick – a gap to a railing – had been set up the opposite way from usual. Still, to Martyn, that wasn't an issue either. He had jumped that railing, in that direction, loads of times previously. Except, this time, Martyn lost his balance. When he tried to rest his foot on the railing he slipped and fell about nine feet. As he dropped, his legs clipped a box, which must have set him in an awkward position during the fall because the impact, when he landed, broke his back.

When I heard of his accident I was devastated. It was hard to see him in such a hellish situation afterwards, though there was a glimmer of hope for us at the beginning. Sometimes, people can get lucky. They break their back in a nasty accident but escape permanent spinal damage. In this case, Martyn seemed to know from the outset, but he was also relieved his fall hadn't carried greater consequences.

'I was immediately just so grateful,' he told *Bike* magazine. 'I just felt lucky, you know? I nearly killed myself. But I hadn't, so I felt really chuffed, to be honest.'

Martyn was in hospital for quite a while. Following an accident of that severity, it's important the injury is allowed to stabilize, because it gives doctors plenty of time to assess the full damage. During that period, a patient is not allowed to move, which must have been a nightmare for Martyn, but that wasn't going to halt his scheming. During one visit, he told me that a crazy idea had come to him. 'I want to finish *Road Bike Party 2*,' he said. 'And I want you to do the final scenes.'

For anyone unfamiliar with the original *Road Bike Party*, it was a legendary film from 2012 where the stunts were performed on a fully carbon road cycle. Put it this way, these bikes are just not built to take the stresses of trials riding.

The carbon frames, the flimsy wheels, the gearing systems are all designed for out-and-out speed, *not* for doing five-feet drops and back flips. This is probably what made Martyn's original film *Road Bike Party* so mind-blowing. Martyn curved around a 'wall of death' (one of those vertical, cylindrical structures that motorcyclists race around at circuses) and back-flipped over a golf-course bunker on a £10,000 bicycle identical to the one used by Sir Bradley Wiggins when he had cleaned up on the Tour de France that same year. Martyn had been halfway through the sequel. Now he wanted me to help him finish the work, which was also going to feature Chris Akrigg. Meanwhile, *Road Bike Party 2* was being made by Robin Kitchen, Martyn's close pal and film-maker.

I was stoked, if a little nervous. I hadn't ridden any lines on a road bike before, not that I was going to let my inexperience bother me. I wanted Martyn to find some focus away from his injury. I told him that I was up for getting involved, which is when he revealed an embarrassing condition to my appearing in the film.

'Danny, I want you to look like me,' he said. 'And if people are gonna believe that you're a proper roadie, you'll have to wear proper shorts.'

If anyone else had suggested the idea of wearing Lycra, I would have said, 'No chance. Forget it.' But this was Martyn. How could I possibly turn him down? It was going to be tricky. I usually rode in jeans. It's what I'd been used to all my life, and I could get away with it in my style of riding because the bottoms didn't get torn up in the chain. Wearing a pair of skimpy shorts was going to be a little disconcerting, but Martyn hadn't finished. It was about to get much, much worse.

'Oh, and shave your legs and slap some fake tan on, too, mate,' he said. 'That way you'll look as if you've been in Lycra all your life. It'll seem more legit for the viewer that way . . .'

These minor editorial details made me feel a little squeamish, but I figured, Well, Martyn's a close mate, and he's having a crap time. I'll go with it . . . I was so keen on helping him to push *Road Bike Party 2* over the line that I would have taken on just about any challenge – even 'man-scaping' my legs and dying them an unusual shade of tangerine.

I started racking my brains for ideas on what I was going to do on the shoot, wondering what on earth I was going to ride on a road bike. In the back of my mind, I remembered a concrete loop-the-loop I had previously seen which had been designed as an art structure and placed outside the Manchester Velodrome. For a while I'd been thinking about doing a project there for GoPro, but it seemed perfect for *Road Bike Party 2*. I was also pretty confident I could pull it off on a different bike, especially after the loop in *Imaginate*. As far as I knew, not even a BMXer had attempted the concrete loop before, although I am sure a few had considered it. Still, I was excited to be giving it a go myself, but perhaps not so enthused at hitting it on a skinny, wee road bike.

First, though, it was decided that I had to ride across the metal tied arches of a wind-whipped bridge in West Yorkshire. It had a fair-sized fall down to a fast-moving river on one side and a twenty-foot drop to the road on the other, so holding a line across it would be risky. But I was up for it and, twenty-four hours before the long drive down, I went into the bathroom with a pair of razors – men's and women's – and started grooming my legs. I lathered up my shins, the blade hacking through the hair, and even though I'd gathered some handy tips from girlfriends, I still managed to slice my flesh to pieces.

There was another dilemma: once I'd shaved above my knee, where was I supposed to stop? One part of me wanted to create a hairy pair of shorts but, seeing as I was in character as a proper roadie, I decided to go further. Only my eyebrows escaped what would prove to be a fairly shoddy attempt at grooming. I also bailed out of the tanning process, despite the bottle of St Tropez I'd bought to slap across my legs. My excuse was the riding. I figured my bronzed shins would begin to streak once I got sweaty.

But man, it felt weird. I drove down to Yorkshire early the next morning in my van, and it was cold. By the time I'd clambered to the top of the bridge, dressed in Lycra, my legs were freezing. A shaving rash burned across my thighs, and the goose bumps only made matters worse. I don't know how roadies make it through the winter in their skimpy shorts. I was in agony.

I was also a little unnerved by the frame. Road bikes (and for my parts I was using a Colnago C59 disc) are designed to stick to the tarmac in high-speed races but, whenever I'd seen someone lose it in the Tour de France, it had always finished with an ugly tangle of limbs at the end. The bike tended to explode into millions of tiny carbon pieces, with broken wheels and cracked handlebars. They definitely weren't designed for the high-impact riding I would be doing during shooting. Martyn's Colnago felt ready to snap even when I was merely testing it around a nearby car park.

In the end, the bridge shot was completed painlessly, but the Velodrome loop was a slightly stickier experience because, to get it right, I required a long run-in, especially if I was to hit the bottom of the sculpture at high speed. I needed the ground to be dry. The loop had been positioned on a grassy area, so to pick up any velocity we would need to build a makeshift track from chipboard, which could be picked up from a nearby DIY shop. Beyond that, my concern was the possibility of my loop attempt being spotted. Any passer-by could capture the whole thing on camera and upload it to YouTube, so our timing had to be perfect.

Our first effort took place shortly after the shooting in West Yorkshire that October, but any hopes for a quick getaway were immediately botched when a thick, soupy fog descended on Manchester. It was impossible to film anything. Robin and I returned a month later, and the weather delivered a gleaming, freezing winter's morning. The conditions were just about perfect for filming.

As you can probably tell by now, I tend to take a ton of run-ups before every banger, to get myself together before throwing myself off the edge or, in this case, around the loop. Prior to arriving at the loop, I had been constantly visualizing what I had to do and thinking how it would feel to tell Martyn I'd done it. But there was something about the shape and size of the Velodrome sculpture that meant there was no hesitating this time: I knew I could do it. It helped that I was trying it for *Road Bike Party 2*, and Martyn. Psychologically, I seemed in a better shape to go at any lines, because it wasn't *my* video, even though the loop was a couple of feet bigger than the one I'd used for *Imaginate*. My only worry was being sucked round into another rotation of the loop. Coming out of the side didn't faze me, but the thought of heading back round without the speed was less than ideal. Falling from the top would be very painful.

As soon as Robin had set up his camera, I looked down to check I was in the right gear, took a breath, shouted 'OK' and set off towards the sculpture. I bombed into the concrete transition, my feet gripping the pedals, my hands white-knuckled on the drops and my chest braced for impact. To be honest, at that point, I had no idea what was going to happen but, sure enough, I was around the loop. If only I'd kept my cool. I was so hyped I'd made it round on my first attempt that I slammed on the brakes and put my feet to the floor rather than just cruising away. That meant the clip was unusable. But buzzing at the realization that the loop was going to work on a road bicycle, I moved into position for another run, though the next attempt didn't quite go to plan. I carved into the pipe too hard and my front tyre squirmed off the rim, jamming into the fork. I lurched over the handlebars, falling fourteen feet and then slammed my shoulder into the concrete, splitting my helmet as I hit the deck.

I was in one piece. Unbelievably, so was the bike. I stuck another tube in the front tyre and went at it again, scything around the concrete curve and shooting out the other side before cruising away as if it had been the easiest trick in the book. As far as I knew, nobody had looped the Velodrome sculpture on any bike before, let alone a road racer, in Lycra, with shaved legs, sporting some brutal rashes and sore thighs. It had been a raw stunt with a limited amount of run-ups; I hadn't used practice mats either.

Manchester was the final scene in *Road Bike Party 2*, so all that was left to be done was the editing. Martyn was chuffed when I called him to deliver the news. He thanked me for sticking through the shoot and helping him to finish the project. That was so important at a crucial moment in Martyn's life. After everything he'd given me throughout his career – the inspiration, the encouragement, as well as the friendship – it was the least I could have done.

Scene Seventeen

<u>FADE IN</u>

(<u>EXT.</u>) A DERELICT STREET IN EPECUÉN,
ARGENTINA

Pablo Novak, the last remaining inhabitant of the
once-flooded town of Epecuén, is cycling through
the streets. We see a scene of devastation around
him. There are caved-in buildings; the roads are
peppered with the detritus of disaster. Tons of
twisted steel and shattered brickwork scatter the
horizon. We zoom in to the squeaking pedals of
Pablo's old bike. The frame is rusted. Over the
noise, we hear his voice . . .

PABLO: In 1985 the rains came . . .

The camera pans back. We see Pablo's dog
running alongside him.

PABLO: The water from the lake rose through the
streets. The town lay beneath the water and with
time was forgotten. Many years later, the water
subsided, uncovering our town. I no longer see
what use this place has for us now . . .

The camera pans back again, the frame filled
with the abandoned city landscape. Pablo rides
into the distance.

                                    Epecuén, 2014

VILLA DE EPECUEN

MATADERO

Tire Tap over Door

Front flip off SeeSaw

flowing gaps Between Building?

17. *Matadero*

I heard about Epecuén in 2012, during the making of *Imagin-ate*. It came about by luck. I'd been researching some potential ideas online, searching for unusual locations. Often, during my sessions on Google Images, I'd type in something like 'Most colourful towns in the world', or 'un-usual architecture', before scrolling through pages of photos. One day, I entered 'abandoned cities' and Epecuén popped up. A town of ruins just over 400 miles south of Buenos Aires in Argentina, it seemed to emerge from a watery land-scape like a lost city in the TV show *Game of Thrones*. The images blew me away. Every picture resembled an apocalyp-tic scene. The buildings were in bits, and all the vegetation was dead. Even the trees were petrified. Bleached white, they rose from the ground like twisted, skeletal fingers.

Epecuén carried quite a story, too. The town (former population 5,000) had been flooded in 1985 when heavy rains filled a nearby lagoon, causing it to burst its banks. Water seeped into the area, once a bustling spa resort, submerging it for twenty-five years. When the flood receded during a drought, the outline of the town was revealed, with everything coated in salt and silt, which gave the place a silvery-white sheen. A quarter of a century after disappearing from view, Epecuén looked eerie, but I could still see a ton of cool lines to check out. There was even an old building, two storeys tall and teetering on the brink of collapse. It had '*Matadero*' affixed to the side in large stone lettering. It means 'slaughterhouse', for those who don't speak Spanish, like me.

'How have I not heard of this place before?' I said. 'I need to get on to this before someone else does.'

I have an irrational thought process whenever I discover a brilliant new location like Epecuén. My first reaction is to think, So who else *might* want to go there? A location is like a banger: once a new trick, or place, has been caught on film, it's done, and a repeat visit by another biker rarely carries the same impact. (Like that loop at the Manchester Velodrome.) The surprise value diminishes. The good news was that I knew a lot of bikers wouldn't consider Epecuén. Skateboarders were out, too. The terrain would be too rough, impractical. But there was nothing stopping someone from making a parkour video in the ruins.

Imaginate had taken ages to complete, with a seemingly endless deadline. Nobody from Red Bull was rushing us to finish. We needed to wrap only once Stu and myself were satisfied that we'd done the job to the best of our abilities.

That allowed us to cling on to the footage for as long as we wanted, and it dragged on. Once we'd finally completed it in Glasgow in April 2013, I told Red Bull I was keen to work on something with a more rigid schedule: a project where I lived on location, filmed solidly for two weeks, and then headed home.

When they asked me if I had a place in mind, I nodded.

'I have, actually,' I said. 'It's called Epecuén.'

I had become obsessed with the town, reading up on the buildings and people; I dug around for articles on its history. The photos from its glory days were spectacular; the spa resembled a holidaymakers' paradise in the 1960s. There were glamorous types hanging around the water in bikinis and skimpy shorts, a bit like a resort on the Côte d'Azur – and definitely not like Dunvegan harbour.

Epecuén was a ghost town in every sense of the word, and the folk living there in 1985 had moved on, apart from one lone-wolf farmer. A weather-beaten old dude called Pablo Novak, he spent his days patrolling the town's rubble and herding his goats.

'I thought before I died I would rebuild this place,' he said in one documentary. 'But I was wrong . . .'

Aside from Pablo, there was plenty of character amidst the broken-up stonework, though Epecuén's backstory caused me to worry a bit. Nobody was killed, but a whole community had been forced to abandon their homes, taking their possessions with them. People had to relocate. Business owners lost their livelihoods. It would have been a traumatic experience for all of them. I guess it helped that over a quarter of a century had passed since the waters first came in, but I was conscious of the people who had once owned the buildings I was planning on riding over.

I wanted to tell their story, so a movie based solely on lines and tricks was a no-go. The best way forward was to deliver an unusual documentary. Every part had to carry an epic mood, matching the town's eeriness, its end-of-days vibe.

I wanted to make something spectacular.

When I finally arrived in Argentina in March of 2014, with Dave Sowerby as my director, I knew we'd found the perfect spot. The *matadero* came into view first, sticking out of the dusty horizon like a mangled fist as we drove towards Epecuén. The abandoned landscape was more surreal than any photo. Dead trees, all of them withered and white, bordered a dirt road that fed into the centre of town. It was midday when we arrived and the sun was beating down, but the intense, forty-degree heat delivered a real beauty, despite the lifeless scenes ahead. In the fierce sunlight, every colour, every surface, looked incredible.

Up close, Epecuén had a powerful atmosphere, a city in ruins; lives had been shattered by the floods, but the devastation meant that there were unusual lines everywhere I looked ... high walls, old window ledges, flat rooftops. There was a derelict playground with seesaws and swings, and old railings that I could gap and ride along. Even the debris offered cool ramp-making material, like rusting steel girders and crumbling breezeblocks. The only downside was the soft terrain. Because everything had been covered in silt, that chalky remnant from the withdrawing lagoon waters, cutting about on a bike was perilous. The ground was gooey; it wobbled like jelly. When I raced through the streets for the first time, just getting enough speed up to make a jump seemed like hard work, and at times the sediment grabbed at my tyres like quicksand. Meanwhile, what was left of the buildings made me think twice about scaling them. Most of the houses were shells. Some of them showed every sign of imminent collapse. Because their foundations and supporting brickwork had been eroded during the floods, each surface would have to be double-checked before I could ride across it.

In the end, we developed what Dave and I were soon referring to as the 'stamp test'. A reckless assessment job, it involved us walking along a rooftop, or ledge, while stomping our feet. At first, we would start gently, with a toe tap. Once we realized that we were standing on a fairly stable structure, the pair of us would then leap up and down as hard as we could, praying that the brickwork didn't fall away and bury us alive under a mountain of rubble. George and John had travelled with us (as 'health and safety inspectors') to help out with some of the structural issues that might come with filming in a derelict town; it was their job to set up my ramps and secure the lines before any riding started. Often they would reinforce ceilings inside the buildings

with junk that was lying around the place, like old steel girders, or a support tower of stone and debris.

There were other helping hands. On arriving in Argentina, we met up with a fixer for the trip, a local dude called
Manu who acted as our translator while we stayed in the
nearby town of Carhué, a spot that now housed some of
Epecuén's former residents. We figured he was somebody
who might be able to hook us up with a key character in
Epecuén's story: the mythical Pablo Novak. From what I
could tell, Pablo didn't speak a word of English, but he was
such an important character in the town's backstory that we
needed him in the video somewhere. Pablo had helped his
neighbours as the floodwaters came in, loading their possessions into cars. He had lived on a goat farm, which was
positioned just above the tide line. His property had been
safe, but he wasn't going to look on as the community
around him disappeared under water.

Pablo had what a lot of people would call 'character'. His
face was tanned and leathered. Deep wrinkles marked his
brow and his grey hair was hidden under a flat cap. For an
eighty-three-year-old, he was in pretty good shape and, whenever his photographs flashed up online, there was generally
one of three activities taking place: Pablo on a beaten-up
shopping bike, Pablo walking down a deserted street (followed by a couple of dogs), or Pablo slurping on a cup of *mate*,
a traditional South American caffeine drink, which is sipped
from a calabash gourd – a strange cup that resembles a smok-
ing pipe. He later told me it was brewed from ground leaves,

like tea. When I first tried *mate* in Carhué, I had a job not to spit it out. My taste buds were assaulted.

A couple of days into the trip we stumbled across Pablo for the first time while we were driving to Epecuén in a pick-up. He came out of nowhere. Through the window, I could see a figure meandering in the distance. It was Pablo, heading towards us on his old bicycle, a dog scampering alongside him, just like in one of those photos. Ahead of him was a herd of goats, and I watched Pablo disappearing into the distance, wondering if we'd see him again.

We were lucky enough to meet him forty-eight hours later. Dave and I were deciding on suitable locations for riding, checking buildings and structures for any risk of death, performing those stamp tests on the concrete. A lot of the time, I could see the internal boundaries, the walls defining the rooms below. That gave me an obvious path to walk, but there were still occasions when the terracotta tiles that covered most of the houses nearly gave way. The salt from the lagoon waters had made everything so brittle that each time I rode across a building for the first time the thought of it collapsing lurked unpleasantly.

That's when we met Pablo. He was on his own version of the 'Wee Commuty', a bicycle that had obviously been underwater for a very long time, and he was herding his goats from one part of town to another. But upon seeing us, he stopped suddenly, bringing the wheels to a halt with a footjam (his brakes were broken). Smiling, I peered down at him from a crumbling ledge; Pablo peered back with an inquisitive expression.

I think he must have marked us down as being – well, a bit mad. Pablo had explored Epecuén from top to bottom. He knew exactly how dangerous it could be to play amidst the rubble, where even the tiniest of objects, like a nail jutting from a wooden plank, could cause injury. After a brief chat mediated by Manu, he agreed to be interviewed. I think the idea that somebody was doing something positive on Epecuén appealed to him. Our angle seemed much better than that of other documentary makers who might ghoulishly dwell on disaster.

When Pablo returned to see us a few days later, he arrived in memorable fashion. George and myself were strengthening an old building, putting up some supporting rebar to prevent a ceiling from caving in. Out of nowhere, a deep thundering reverberated between the crumbling walls. I looked at George, and the pair of us scrambled outside to take a look. It was Pablo, driving towards us in his jeep, emerging from a giant ball of dust.

Talk about making a scene! Pablo's 'car' was a real beast, an old jeep that had been salvaged from the flood waters, rebuilt by his son and had the presence of a Mad Max vehicle. The exhaust had fallen off, which was the reason for all that noise. Meanwhile, the bonnet had been removed and a piece of tarpaulin had been stretched over the top in its place. Pablo had to start the engine by hotwiring the ignition with a screwdriver. But makeshift living was what he did best: when Pablo sat down to chat in his house, a bric-a-brac construction of junk and scrap metal, he told us how he had to adapt once the water came in.

'The flooding process started back in 1980,' he said. 'The lagoon started flooding. It grew and grew, so we created a defence. We worked for four years with the defence. It looked uncertain, as sometimes it worked and sometimes it didn't. We didn't think the water would come in any more, but it continued to rise, until one morning it blew up.'

Pablo had been determined to stay. He was born in Villa Epecuén, a son to one of the town's founders, and when we met him he had been a resident all his life. 'The moving process lasted close to a month,' he told us. 'On 16 November 1985, we started, and after that we worked for another sixteen days underwater. We had quite some time because, if it had all blown up on that day, we would not have been able to get anything out. Everyone was working together, and the people in Carhué were all cooperating. We did not leave much behind – a few things from the government, some vehicles, but nothing major . . .'

At times, retelling the tragedy caused him to stare off into the distance. I knew his voice would bring the tale of Epecuén to life.

There wasn't a sense of any impending doom when I'd first decided to jump from the '*Matadero*' sign. But standing at the top, with a thirteen-foot drop to the roof below, and another thirty foot of falling distance beneath that (should the brickwork cave in when I landed), gave me a little rush of fear. The wheels of my bike rested on the stone letters, the front on the D, my back tyre perched along the E; the surface was probably no wider than two feet. I knew that if I fell from that height I wouldn't be in for a good time. Meanwhile, John was stressing a bit in the courtyard below. He stared up at me, a nervy expression on his face. He had filmed with a ton of riders, during a lot of crazy projects, but I'd never known him to look this worried. We both realized my starting position was a little exposed (there was a forty-two-foot drop to the other side of the sign), but his anxiety wasn't going to stop me from dropping off the edge. To make things worse, we had a drone in the air to capture the drop, which made communication with Dave very difficult. As soon as I'd clocked that first photograph of the *matadero* on my laptop, I knew I'd have to scale it in some way.

I hopped on to my back wheel, locking my back brake right on the edge, and lowering my front wheel so my bike was horizontal. I moved forward, leaving the letter 'D' behind and falling to the concrete below. To my surprise, the brick-work held strong. Miraculously, I wasn't asphyxiating in a tomb of dust and old brick, but as I tried to kick on the momentum I'd needed to jump to the next wall slipped away on impact. I was gutted. The take was scrapped. A couple of minutes later, I was up on the lettering again, the sun was beating down on us, and I was unsure if I had another drop in me. And the drone was making above me clear communication impossible. At times, I wasn't sure whether Dave was saying 'Go!' or 'No!' I wasn't going to let it unsettle me, though. On the third take, I nailed the landing, riding away in one piece before gapping a series of ledges that took me down to ground level. From there, I cascaded through the back of the building, eventually dropping out of a window and into what had once been a busy road. I was buzzing.

We had been filming in Epecuén for ten days, and I knew the *matadero* part had been big, something special, but we still needed a banger to finish the piece. We had tirelessly scoured the area for a line that was big enough to do it. We didn't find one. So, pulling an idea that I had previously saved for my future mountain-bike edit, *The Ridge*, I decided on a front bump flip, a stunt with a heck of a lot of technique. But first, I'd have to carve up a makeshift ramp. As my bike left the ground, the plan was for my front wheel to 'bump' (in reality, smash) into another object positioned in front – a wall, say, or in this case, a road sign stuck to a post. With the momentum of the front wheel striking the sign, I could flip myself over 360 degrees before I landed and rode away, hopefully without any broken bones or shattered teeth.

That's the theory, anyway. The reality required plenty of practice, and I could not get it right. We'd brought a bunch of crash mats with us, but my success rate was pretty low. I would hit the road sign and flip over without too much stress but, often, I'd land on my back. For a while, I thought the trick wasn't going to happen.

After I'd finished riding the *matadero*, one of the most epic days of shooting I'd ever done, I dropped my bike and tried to relax. I was knackered, it was pretty late in the day and all the lines on that old building had taken their toll; we had been on location from sunrise to sunset. Epecuén seemed to throw up such a brilliant light that it was proving a dream location for Dave, and everything he captured turned out incredibly well, but we needed a banger to close the video. We both knew the bump front flip was exactly that, I just had to get my head straight, so I sat down in the dust as the sun began setting over the lake. A cluster of heavy-looking clouds had gathered in the distance. The lagoon was starting to darken.

'Danny, you know, if the light were to break through,' said Dave, 'it would be the perfect moment to capture this last stunt . . .'

I knew he was right, but at that moment it seemed almost impossible. The trick, I guessed, might cause me to hurt myself. Meanwhile, everyone was rushing around, just in case I decided to go for it. The cameras were in place. Everybody was primed but, because the sun was fading, our equipment was operating to its limits. If the sky got any darker, the onscreen images would turn grainy.

I ignored the chaos around me and grabbed my phone. All day, I'd been listening to a track called 'Calm Down' by an indie band named The Love Language, and the guitars had helped me to focus. I glanced across at the sign one last time. It was sticking up in the ground, positioned in front of George and John's 'ramp' – a jagged concrete pillar . . . The clouds broke, just slightly, a sliver of sunlight burning through the horizon. It was now or never.

I grabbed the bike and went at the jump, cutting up the ramp as fast as I could. My front wheel took off, nudging into the sign, and as I spun over the top, everything whirled around me – tyres, sign, air, ground . . . the trees ahead. *Crunch!* I landed and spun away, my wheels curling through the mud and rock. I was in one piece and super-stoked.

I hate talking about firsts, and there have been a few in my videos, but landing a bump front flip seemed extra special, more so than the *matadero* or my flip over the wall at Edinburgh Castle. Why? Well, nobody had ever done one in a riding film before – not on a trials frame, anyway. With that one-take trick in Epecuén, we'd made a banger with a difference.

Not that Mother Nature seemed too impressed. Those moody clouds had suddenly swept inland. The sky darkened and strong winds whipped and whistled through the buildings. I heard Robbie shout, 'It's coming!' And in seconds, our excited, jubilant mood was transformed into a mad panic. Crash mats and camera equipment blew across the ground. A tent we'd put up, our shelter from the sun, threatened to take off in the squall, and the town was engulfed in a wall of dust. Nobody could breathe. Epecuén was telling us to leave.

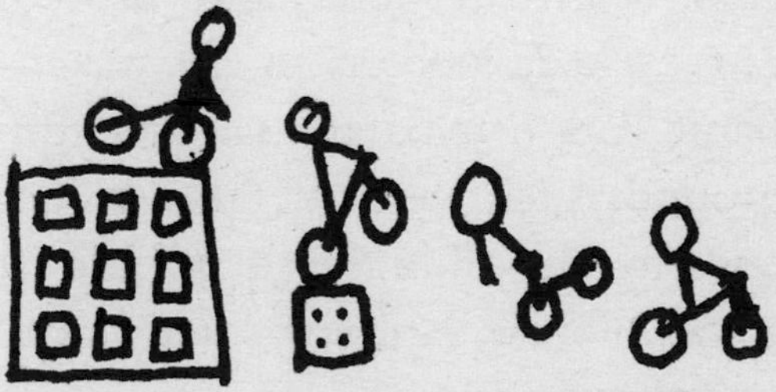

Scene Eighteen

<u>FADE IN</u>

(<u>EXT.</u>) The Playboy Mansion grounds, Beverly Hills

In close-up, three Playboy playmates stride along a path that leads into the Playboy Mansion. We zoom back up and see the grounds and house, complete with opulent fountains and medieval-looking turrets.

Danny's bike carves into view. He hops over the water fountain on the main drive, startling the three girls, who turn quickly to check the cause of the noise. Danny pulls a fake nose manual on the lawn. His next move is to tyre-tap 270 on to a bench, jump over a hedge and drop ten feet into a tennis court below where two girls are playing a match. One of them tries to hit him with a racquet. Danny evades them, hopping over the net and riding away . . .

Danny MacAskill
At The Playboy Mansion, 2014

Tire Tap Into Tennis Court

180 Over Net

Bunny

Front Flip Into Harour

Over Boat

18. Pool Parties

I wasn't interested in launching my films with fancy premieres or parties. Yes, there had been a fairly big party for *Imaginate* at the time, but that was with the friends who had been involved in its making. For the release of *Inspired Bicycles* and *Industrial Revolutions*, the celebrations were low key. I invited a bunch of mates to my Edinburgh flat, ordered some food, my pal Iain Withers brought a bag full of champagne, some Jägermeister and a few beers, but it was a tame affair. We watched the film a handful of times and uploaded the video on to YouTube before settling in for a marathon of *Family Guy*.

These days, the launch of a new video is a slightly more extravagant event. Once *Epecuén* had been delivered, Red Bull decided they wanted to launch it with a series of lavish events, all of which were more head-spinning than a bump front flip over a rusty road sign. I was flown to their HQ in LA for a screening, which was followed by a surprise trip to the Playboy Mansion. (I'll talk you through that ill-fated adventure in a minute.) Another launch was organized to take place at the X-Games, the world-renowned action-sports festival. It was being held in Austin, Texas, and it was a pretty big deal, with the US broadcaster ESPN screening it every year.

If a trip to the States to promote *Epecuén* seemed a little over the top to me, I hadn't appreciated Red Bull's ambition. They decided we should celebrate *Epecuén*'s release at a party in Monte Carlo, slap-bang in the middle of the 2014 Formula 1 Grand Prix in Monaco, one of the most glamorous events on the sporting calendar. It was quite the contrast to Epecuén. Because Red Bull had an F1 team of their own, the owners took a 'floating palace' to the harbour where they could entertain friends and business partners, such as the drivers, their families, and wealthy and influential movers within F1. It was about as far removed from my normal, day-to-day life as you could possibly imagine.

Named *The Energy Station*, the party venue dwarfed most of the super-yachts in the harbour. A slick bar called the Mediterranean Terrace was on the top deck, and there was a swimming pool, white leather sofas and sunshades. Red Bull even had a lavish speedboat which transported several elite guests to and from their yachts, and that included myself and Tarek. It was a cool way to travel and definitely the way to arrive in style. *The Energy Station* was mind-blowing. All I could think was, What is this? And how the hell has my trials bike brought me here?

Everywhere I looked, there was a famous face. At home, my blending into the shadows could often border on an art form (when I wasn't riding around, of course), but I ended up chatting to some really cool names in Monaco, such as Maxi Jazz. He was a rapper from Faithless, a band who had inspired me so much when I rode around the Gun Shop in Dunvegan. There was also Reggie Bush Jr, running back for the Detroit Lions, and Michael Carrick of Manchester United. It was also cool to hang out with the F1 star-turned-TV presenter David Coulthard and Red Bull Racing driver Daniel Ricciardo.

Despite preparing for a big championship, Daniel was still keen on having a go on my bike. He had a bit of style about him, too, and while cutting about on the Mediterranean Terrace he did a few stoppies and wheelies. I noticed that a few of the Red Bull crew were firing some anxious looks his way. Then I remembered the story about Mark Webber, another one of their drivers. He had broken his shoulder in 2010 after stacking it on a mountain bike, just before the Japanese Grand Prix. The fact that this had happened while messing around on two wheels hadn't gone down well – not with the folks at Red Bull Racing, anyway. I realized that a repeat incident on *The Energy Station*, *on my bike*, would have been less than ideal, but it was nice to see that Daniel couldn't care less.

I was under no such limits, however, and I think it was during a visit to the Mediterranean Terrace that somebody first suggested the idea of me doing a front flip off the side of the *Energy Station* into the sea. 'You know, if Daniel Ricciardo managed to get on the podium this weekend . . .' was the suggestion. Talk about a red rag to a bull. I wasn't the first Red Bull athlete to be riding on the *Energy Station* during the F1. The freerunner Ryan Doyle had performed there last year, as had my moto trials hero, Dougie Lampkin. He had jumped over the swimming pool on his trials motorbike.

I did a few small shows for the guests on the *Energy Station*, using the red ball from *Imaginate*, a bunny-hop bar and a wee kicker positioned so I could back-flip across the pool. After these shows were done, I spoke to one of the Red Bull team about possibly leaning a board against one of the railings at the top of the second storey of the barge. I wanted to race up it and front-flip into the harbour. I got a funny look at first but, before I knew it, somebody had found a wooden board from below, presumably stripped from a fancy mahogany lounge. I was pleased. A set-up like that sounded pretty cool. At the very least, I'd have an interesting photo to hang on my bathroom wall afterwards.

Of course, Daniel made it to the podium, finishing third, behind Nico Rosberg and Lewis Hamilton, and so, that same afternoon, my jump was locked in. The ramp was wedged against the side of *The Energy Station*, the clear blue waters of Monaco harbour twinkling below. Positioned in the sea, kicking back in a special boat moored just underneath us, was Reggie Bush Jr, but I wasn't fussed by my high-profile audience. Riding a floating party palace in Monaco was a bit surreal. After all, I was just there to launch *Epecuén*, but as I took a run-up past all 'the beautiful people' and the multimillion-dollar yachts whirling around in my sightlines, I thought back to my mates in Glasgow. Duncan Shaw and myself had been planning a new touring trials show called 'Drop and Roll'. I knew he'd been buying the business a new van that day, yet here I was, lording it up in the South of France, jumping off a boat in front of NFL superstars and F1 drivers.

I'm happy to take one for the team, I thought.

I hit the cool water and was submerged.

On the list of sentences I'm unlikely to hear too often, 'Fancy a day messing about in the Playboy Mansion for some pictures?' had to be right up there. I lived in a shared flat in Glasgow with my seven friends. The hallway, bedrooms and living room were a jumble of old frames and tyres. We had Sky TV (though we hardly ever used it), a BBQ and a hot tub, but it was like an inner-city bachelor's pad. Meanwhile, Hugh Hefner's place in Beverly Hills was a symbol of high living. His empire was built around a twenty-two-room home, complete with tennis court, screening room, zoo and a grotto, where one or two steamy parties were reported to have taken place during its heyday. The mansion was some set-up, but I wouldn't trade it for my bit in Glasgow.

I wasn't entirely sure whether being associated with the Playboy brand was my thing. I was unsure of how anyone else in the trials world – and beyond – would take it. The feeling I had was, Well, I'm in LA, I've got this interesting opportunity . . . What would my younger self in the Cave think? I took some comfort in the fact that he would be into it, but only if I managed some good riding. I didn't want the pictures to look cheesy, so I knew I'd have my work cut out. As a biker, you're only as good as the tricks you're landing, wherever you are. I went to Beverly Hills crossing my fingers I'd have enough obstacles to play with.

Once we'd pulled into the grounds, the Playboy Mansion came into view like a miniature castle. There were medieval-looking rooftops, ornate windows, and a fancy water feature positioned in the middle of the driveway. We might have been in sunny California, but Hugh's pad reminded me of a hunting lodge you'd find in the Scottish Highlands. Surrounded by pine trees, the place was secluded from the outside world. No matter where we stood, there wasn't a glimpse of LA, or the skyscrapers and freeways beyond. Hugh wasn't around either, but of course there were Playmates – six glamorous-looking types in bunny outfits and floppy ears.

I wasn't too bothered about the place or the bunnies; my main concern was finding some lines for the shoot. I was still using the Inspired Skye, a frame that Dave Cleaver from *Inspired Bicycles* and myself had spent years perfecting. It seemed ages since we'd first got together in 2007, and since my debut YouTube video in Edinburgh I'd smashed up a lot of his prototypes – a hell of a lot. He tinkered with his blueprints and, by 2014, everything was just about spot on. My frame and fork were sturdy. That meant the bike reacted to whatever I was doing, most of the time.

In the Playboy Mansion, the conditions were not as challenging as the usual stuff. I jumped across the fountain on Hugh's driveway and tyre-tapped from a bench over a bush and into a tennis court, where a couple of Playmates were in the middle of a match. One of them struck me across the backside with her racquet as I whizzed past. After that, I jumped from a bridge over the swimming pool (and a bunch of girls sunbathing below), before pulling a fakie nose manual all the way down Hugh's front lawn. That was a lot of fun, though I'm not sure what the groundskeeper would have made of it. Later that day, I even gapped between two rails above rapper Warren G's head while wrapping up for the day at Red Bull HQ . . . 'Regulators!!'

What I hadn't expected was a backlash. I'd been under the impression that we were doing a photo session to help with the launch of *Epecuén*. It was just a day of shooting, a bit of fun, and very different from anything I'd done before. Of course, I imagined there might be some behind-the-scenes clips to accompany the pictures, but nothing more. So it came as a bit of a shock when a two-minute video of me razzing around the Playboy Mansion appeared on Facebook.

Oh no, I thought. I wasn't expecting this.

The fact there was even footage in circulation had slipped my mind, mainly because I wasn't involved in the editing process, or the musical side, which I was always passionate about.

At first, there were quite a few positive comments from viewers – the downhill and freeride scenes seemed into it. But a mini-storm gathered on some of the forums. A few female riders got upset, and a couple of the big magazines ran negative editorials. There were accusing voices on Twitter.

'We won't be featuring the latest video from @danny_ macaskill on our site,' posted one editor. 'Well, it's 2014 and not the 1980s.'

I could see their points of view. At the time, the first edition of La Course by the Tour de France was taking place, an elite race for women pro cyclists. Equality was an issue in all aspects of cycling, so I understood why my working in the Playboy Mansion had upset a lot of people, though it was an honest mistake on my part. The brand's image may have crossed my mind when I'd first got to the house. I knew about its rep back in the day, but Playboy had opened a few high-street stores in the States since then, so I'd assumed it wasn't that offensive any more. (Hands up, I was wrong.) Besides, slicing about the grounds for some photos had been a light-hearted move, nothing more. It wasn't my intention to offend.

For a couple of days I sucked up the flak and dusted myself down. I knew my integrity had taken a slight dent, but I reassured myself with the fact that I was midway through the editing of another video, one that had brought my filming a little closer to home – to Skye, in fact, where I had been working with Stu again. I'd dreamt of racing along some epic terrain for years, one that matched adventure and technical riding with amazing scenery and –

Click! I had a theme and a location which twinned epic views with exposed trails, and it meant one thing: I was taking on the Black Cuillins, the ridgeback mountains that dominated Skye's breathtaking landscape. Forget the Playboy Mansion, I was going back to my roots.

Scene Nineteen

<u>FADE IN</u>

(<u>EXT.</u>) Loch Scavaig, the Black Cuillins
Mountains, on the Isle of Skye

We hear the rippling of water. We see an oar; a
shot of Danny's shoes. He's sitting in a boat,
rowing slowly towards the shoreline. A seal
stirs from his spot on a nearby rock and dives
into the sea. It begins to follow Danny's trail.

DANNY: Growing up on Skye, the Black Cuillins for
me have always been an inaccessible place.
There's an incredible knife-edge ridge that runs
right across the top of them and I've always
wondered if it would be possible to ride my
mountain bike up there . . .

Cut to a drone camera, which is flying towards
Danny. We see the dark, inky water below him,
his boat, and the ominous-looking Black Cuillins
Mountains beyond, swathed in white cloud . . .

The Ridge, 2014

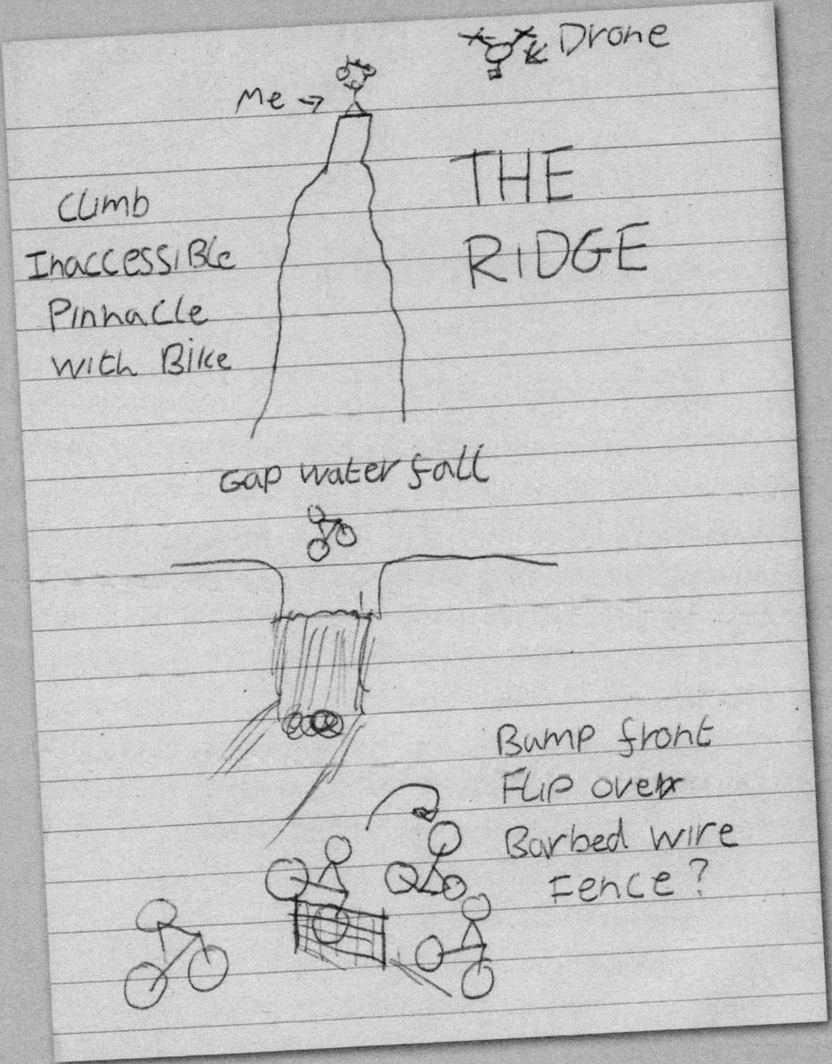

Drone

Me →

Climb
Inaccessible
Pinnacle
With Bike

THE
RIDGE

Gap water fall

Bump front
Flip over
Barbed wire
Fence?

19. The Inaccessible Pinnacle

As a kid, I gazed up at the Black Cuillins Mountains in awe. Seventeen dark peaks, eleven Munros and seven and a bit miles of craggy ridgeline. I only had to leave my front door and stroll down the road, and there they were, rising out of the Skye horizon like pieces of jagged slate. In the summer, when the sun reflected off the black igneous rock that covered the landscape, they turned a deep purple. In winter, the peaks were swathed in snow and brooding cloud, like a miniature version of the Alps. At the summit: the Inaccessible Pinnacle, a lethally thin razorblade of rock.

You had to be a serious mountaineer to make it to the very top and, as kids, we'd heard that the terrain up there was very tricky, some of the most challenging in the UK, especially when the weather blew in, which it could at a moment's notice. That's probably why I never came close to venturing up when I was younger. Sometimes I went to the river at the bottom with friends, to play in the 'Fairy Pools' in Glen Brittle – several rocky shallows and waterfalls that had formed among the inlets, but that was as far as we would dare venture. Even a reckless kid like me knew there was danger attached to whatever was happening further along the path.

That's not to say I didn't love it around there. Whenever I travelled to the base of the mountain I'd marvel at how the Cuillins stretched up into the sky. Frothing white clouds swirled around the peaks. In summer, seals played in clear blue waters near the sandy beaches and, as you wandered inland on a narrow trail, the vegetation became dotted with pink, red and yellow flowers. It was just about the perfect place to make a riding film.

I'd first considered cutting about on the Cuillins a couple of years earlier, during the making of *Way Back Home*, but I worried that the visual impact of the Inaccessible Pinnacle might not fit with our shots at Edinburgh Castle, or in Dunvegan and Raasay. Also, the slog required just to scale the Inaccessible Pinnacle (or 'In-Pin', as we called it) warranted a bigger project. The path up included a climb of three thousand feet and, with equipment, that would take some work. As if that wasn't bad enough, certain chunks of that route were a scramble, others involved proper rock climbing, and the gradient for walking was much steeper than forty-five degrees. It was pretty full on.

Once Stu and myself had settled on making a video on a mountain bike rather than a trials frame, we figured it might be better to gather together the help of my other sponsors, such as 5-10, who provided me with shoes, and the mountain-bike manufacturers Santa Cruz, rather than operating under the umbrella of any huge brands, like Red Bull, or a camera company such as GoPro. I'd spent so much of my time gallivanting around Epecuén and Monaco on my Inspired that I knew I'd feel rusty working on a mountain bike. My concern was that some of the riding might seem a little stiff. I also knew it would take me a while to get used to the dynamics of a mountain bike, which was a lot harder for the gaps and hops required to clear the rivers I planned on working my way across. Because this was my first proper mountain-bike film, if the parts didn't pan out as well as we'd hoped, we could shelve the footage and only be wasting our own time. With that in mind, the pair of us block-booked a time schedule for shooting: two weeks in June 2014, when we hoped that – fingers crossed – the weather might behave itself. Listen, it was Scotland: what could possibly go wrong?

Just about everything, in fact. I'd never been to the top of the range so, three weeks prior to our shooting, I went for a recce with Stu, plus a tour guide from Skye Adventure called Matt, an expert on all things Black Cuillins-related. Our plan had been to check out the terrain while scouting for potential shooting locations. But talk about throwing ourselves in at the deep end! As we made our way to the top, the clouds blew in. Rain and high winds battered us from all sides. Mist made it impossible to see anything further than ten feet ahead and there were severe drops to the left and the right, some of them falling away to depths of several hundred feet. The landscape was a shock, too. There were exposed bluffs and awkward ledges to manoeuvre along. It was hard enough on foot, never mind on two wheels. Suddenly, a two-week shoot was beginning to resemble an Ernest Shackleton-style adventure to the Antarctic.

We somehow got through our trek in one piece, and that must have steeled us for the worst. Once Stu, the team and myself had established camp in a rented house in nearby Carbost a few weeks later, all of us felt ready for anything. At first, the weather forecasts made for grim reading: torrential rain, high winds and fog, probably with plagues of midges thrown in. But everything changed in a heartbeat. On the first day of shooting, the skies were set to clear in the afternoon. The weather was warm. For the first of several long treks towards the top of the Black Cuillins, the mood was bouncing.

It was hard work, though. We had to negotiate around two thousand feet of scree, some of us carrying drone cameras, others lugging heavy lights and batteries. I was shifting a lot of gear, too – spare tubes, an extra tyre, some food and, of course, the bike, a Santa Cruz Bronson. To make progress, I utilized the frame in the same style a snowboarder might use their board during a steep, off-piste climb. With one hand holding the fork and the other gripping my seat tube, I attempted to force the wheels into any loose rock ahead. Using them as leverage, I literally had to drag myself up the hill. I must have lifted my frame thousands of times to get to the top of the scree slopes. We were all absolutely knackered.

Our climb, which took us to the trail that meandered along the top of the ridge, was worth it. As we got to a suitable vantage point for filming, the clouds began to break below us; bright blue skies burned overhead. I could see as far out as Rum at one end of the island and Raasay at the other. We didn't want to waste any of the light. Quickly, I got on to the bike as Stu set up his camera equipment, but I felt rusty. I hadn't been on my Santa Cruz all year and everything seemed a little off. As I started to pedal, my riding felt wooden; there was no fluidity. Each push on the pedals began tentatively but, luckily, we were only focusing on some basic trails that afternoon.

Despite my worries, over the next couple of days Stu and the team's cinematography bordered on the epic. In one shot, I rode along the side of Collie's Ledge, a rocky path that was no wider than a foot and a half. If I hadn't carried a good head for heights, that narrow route alone might have given me a heart attack, mainly because there was a sheer drop of several hundred feet to my left. If I were to slip and fall, there would be no coming back. I had to keep my wits about me. I sped along the path, making sure not to clip a pedal or my handlebars on a slice of loose rock.

Meanwhile, as I made my way down, a drone camera buzzed around me, capturing every turn, every twist. At the end of the day, once we'd gathered around Stu's laptop back in Carbost to watch the latest clips, I could tell the film was beginning to come together. We were lucky with the weather, the riding and quality of shots we were working on, but we still couldn't tell if the stuff we were doing was going to amount to anything ground-breaking. We still had a lot of work to do.

The In-Pin beckoned.

I was standing near the top of the Black Cuillins, around two hundred feet from the In-Pin's tallest point. But as I perched precariously on that cliff face, I could only think of one thing – what a view! Skye's razorback ridge cut across the horizon: clouds smoked over the mountaintops; the sun blazed above them. I wanted to gawp at the scene for hours, but I couldn't risk losing an ounce of concentration – not yet. There was a distance of twenty feet to climb. The final reach to the top was precarious, and so I edged carefully along the rocks, my feet and fingers grasping for stability. I was at least a hundred feet up from the next ledge and the only thing holding me from a fatal, ragdoll-style tumble was a climbing rope. Without it, a slip might plunge me to the rocks below.

I could see my bike trailing behind on a winch that was being operated by Stu and the production crew; the remote-controlled drone camera buzzed overhead, capturing the Black Cuillins from above, and my body, now a wee speck on that huge mass of rock. I reached out for my Santa Cruz and pushed ahead. Getting on to the peak had been a dream for years, and when I finally clambered up and clocked the amazing sights of Skye below – the green landscape, the beaches, the sea stretching into the distance – my mind buzzed. I drank it all in. Standing on that three-feet-wide summit, perched on two wheels, was one of the coolest things I'd ever done.

The drone captured it beautifully; on the video, you can see my body silhouetted against the brilliant blue sky. But standing at the top wasn't enough for me; I needed my climb to look legit, because I'd maintained a high level of authenticity in all my films – like *Inspired Bicycles*. I'd hopped up to the edge of that spiky fence from a makeshift jump, rather than climbing on to the top, which would have been a lot easier. In my mind, I had to ride an entire line. It would have bugged me otherwise. The Black Cuillins were no different. I knew that if I could be seen scaling the peak, the bike on my back, it would deliver the credibility I sought. Plus, I didn't want to fool anybody. I'm not into making movies with CGI stunts or high-wire trickery. Everything I put on camera has to be real, though to pull that off I sometimes needed to take risks, and this was one of those occasions. I clambered down for around fifty feet so I could make the final ascent again, but this time with the safety rope unclipped and the Santa Cruz slung over my shoulder. That way, I could capture some clean POV shots from my free climb to the top. I checked my balance and peered apprehensively at the sheer drop below. Once I felt comfortable, I radioed down to Stu.

'I'm just gonna unclip quickly,' I said.

My walkie-talkie crackled straightaway. Stu sounded pretty stressed. 'Dude, keep the rope on!'

I edged forward, my hands and feet scoping out the summit for any loose rock. The pinnacle was still only three feet wide, if that, but I felt pretty stable. I yelled down to Stu. 'This bit's fine,' I said. 'The rope makes it harder for me . . .'

Detaching the rope, I pushed forward. Apparently, the whole crew were very tense. Everybody was focused, but on edge as I made those last few steps across the peak. 'What are you doing?' said Stu tensely. But I could feel the confidence surging through me. I was in control, and I didn't think I was taking a risk, even though there was a hundred-foot drop. Besides, I was on my feet. I would have felt comfy on my bike at that height, and I knew that I could always bin my wheels off the cliff if the worst came to the worst and grab on to the rock face with two hands.

I had experience of this style of climbing, though my previous adventure had been sketchy. Once, I got myself trapped on the side of a cliff when I was around thirteen years old, in probably my closest tango with death. Man, it was hellish. After a day of beachcombing in Trumpan, in north-west Skye, with my friends Andrew and Calum, we had clambered up a sheer face, a two-hundred-foot-tall expanse of rotten rock and loose grass. At the time, we'd thought it would make for a fun route home but, once I got close to the top, it was obvious that the last fifty feet or so were just too treacherous to climb.

It was blowing a hoolie that day, and the buffeting winds were shifting everybody's balance about and drowning out our desperate shouts to one another. Below us, the view was even worse. I could see the ocean, and the water was very turbulent. It crashed around the rocks, whipping up a terrifying, frothing white soup of certain death. I knew I was staring into trouble. My legs started to wobble.

If I climb any further, I'm gonna fall and die, I thought. Or, worse, someone's going to see us, call out the mountain rescue . . . And Mum's going to go mad.

A ferry passed, but it was miles away in the distance, too far to hear our screams. We were in serious trouble.

I realized that if I was to get off that rock alive, I needed to compose myself. I stayed put, assessing the situation. I reached across to find a fresh handhold, but there was nothing I could cling on to for too long – the rock was loose. But if I could spot a ledge, or an OK space, the three of us could huddle together while we waited for someone to find us. We'd have to sleep on the cliff. Then I saw it . . . *There!* A succession of ledges and footholds that might lead us to safety. My confidence started to come back. Carefully, I shifted down to where Calum and Andrew were stuck, before guiding us away to safety.

Once we had dropped down to the beach below, relief hit me in a rush. The three of us were buzzing, happy to still be alive. Calum rummaged around in his rucksack and pulled out three cups and a flask of instant coffee, which he'd warned us was loaded with sugar. Ordinarily, I would have said, 'No, thanks,' because Mum used to drink bitter black coffee at home and I hated the stuff. But sitting on that rocky beach, it was the sweetest thing I'd ever tasted.

Compared to that awful, crumbling cliff face in Trumpan, the In-Pin was a lot more manageable. Everything seemed solid, stable; I edged my way up the gabbro rock, one-handed. With my 5-10 cycling shoes on, I felt like a gecko, and I knew my decision to lose the safety rope had been spot on. If I'd felt unstable or the trembles had kicked in, I wouldn't have gone through with it, especially not with my friends around to see the results of a fall. It wouldn't be right to put them through the stress, though it was easy for me to think that way. My emotions were in a different place to theirs: the heart rate was low, I felt relaxed; everything was under control. It has to be on every stunt I do. Come on, I'm not a madman . . .

For several days, we gathered more clips. I rode across a tree branch positioned across two boulders. The line took me over a babbling stream. Later, I raced along trails of scree, ploughing over any jagged boulders that crossed my path. We even captured some clips of me rowing a boat over Loch Scavaig towards the ominous-looking Black Cuillins, though that part of the filming required a fair helping of smoke and mirrors. Stu wanted to create a solitary vibe. His drone camera swept overhead, revealing the vast expanse of water beneath me and the ridges ahead, all of them swaddled in gloomy cloud. What his footage didn't reveal was the Skye

Boat Trips ferry that had towed me most of the way. After six days, I was wiped out.

By the end of the trip, I couldn't have been happier. Stu's camera had captured Skye in all its beauty and, once we had finished editing, we named our latest work *The Ridge* as a nod to the In-Pin and the Black Cuillins' challenging peaks. It's funny, though: when Stu and I first showed it to a few people, the reaction was underwhelming. Our mates thought it was a fun film. Several sponsors were of the mind-set that it was a nice shoot, and most people commented on the spectacular views. But that was about it, to be honest, and I guess I felt the same way. When we watched *The Ridge* back in its entirety for the first time, we shrugged. It had been a little too easy, especially compared to some of the other stuff we had made.

Everything changed once *The Ridge* had been released on YouTube and Stu's own channel, Cut Media. The online hits went up and up, into the tens of millions, which was unexpected, and, currently, it's the biggest viral we've made to date. The positive comments were also off the scale, and once the BBC had released a 'making of' documentary called *Riding the Ridge*, everybody was talking about us. That was a real thrill. I had wanted to show Skye off as an incredible place (it truly is, by the way – you should go) and, with 43 million YouTube views, hopefully, some of that audience will be inspired enough to go and visit one day. *The Ridge* was a snapshot of home.

Sometimes, when I go back to see my folks now, I'll bump

into tourists claiming they've arrived having seen *The Ridge*. Others have told me they were blown away by our clips of the Black Cuillins Mountains and the 'Fairy Pools'. More tourists in Skye can only be good for the area, especially if they're visiting Dad's Angus MacAskill Museum in Dunvegan. Providing the traffic doesn't get any worse around the village, I'm delighted. We all are.

Scene Twenty

(<u>EXT.</u>) The Glasgow Museum of Transport

Professional rider Martyn Ashton, one of Danny's childhood heroes, arrives at the set of Imaginate, a – so far – top-secret project. The building has been in lock-down for weeks. Martyn is waiting outside. He has no idea of the craziness going on beyond the front doors.

MARTYN: Danny's nuts, he'll try some crazy stuff, so I've got no idea what's gonna be in there. A lot of work's gone into it, so I'm looking forward to going inside. I'm expecting some colour, crazy obstacles. Danny's got a big imagination. He loved the [Michael Jackson] video Billie Jean . . . maybe there are some stairs that light up. Maybe a giraffe?

(<u>INT.</u>) The Glasgow Museum of Transport

Martyn sees the loop-the-loop, Stu's cameras; his eyes scan over the crew, and the crash mats. He looks amazed at the production process . . . Later, he watches as Danny jumps out of a super-sized air vent, down a ramp designed to look like a copy of a *Dandy* annual and around a loop-the-loop.

MARTYN: You are a headcase . . . What the f**k?! That was amazing!

MacAskill's Imaginate, Episode 5, 2013

Start

Colour

20. The Viral Formula

I was aiming to make one big film a year, maybe two.

Inspired Bicycles, *Way Back Home* and *Industrial Revolutions* had done well, some of them clocking up over 30 million hits on YouTube, a number I struggled to get my head around. But once Red Bull had released *Imaginate* and the viewing numbers started going up and up, it became clear that we (and by 'we' I mean the likes of directors Dave Sowerby, Stu Thomson and, later, Robbie Meade, as well as myself) had stumbled on to a bit of a film-making formula. All of us understood what it took to make a successful video, one that stood apart from so many others on the internet.

So, with that in mind, here are a few pointers that have worked for us in the past. They're hardly foolproof, but a few of the ideas here might give you some food for thought, regardless of whatever scene you're in. Some of this stuff might even change your riding style.

The Theme

One of the first things I think of when I'm starting a new project is the theme. It's like an umbrella, and everything – all the lines, filming, locations and music – fits within it. Having a journey or a story in a viral makes it a little more engaging, especially to a mainstream viewer, somebody who might not have watched a street-trials clip before.

You could have a road trip as your theme, or maybe your idea might be a street-trials compilation. The options are endless. So to get you started, here, in order of release, are the themes I've used in my bigger online parts.

- *TartyBikes* – A basic street-trials film set around Aviemore.
- *Inspired Bicycles* – Another street-trials video, but this one was made around Edinburgh; I wanted to push myself further than I'd ever gone before.
- *Way Back Home* – A road trip through Scotland, using the camper as a thread through the whole film, from Edinburgh to Skye, mixing epic backdrops with street trials on abandoned structures like dams, old buildings and red telephone boxes.
- *Industrial Revolutions* – I rode around a disused ironworks, jumping over trains and rusting tracks.
- *Imaginate* – I'm a child's toy come to life, riding around a messy bedroom floor.

- *Epecuén* – Exploring the ruins of a flooded town.
- *The Ridge* – My mountain-bike adventure across the notorious Black Cuillins in Skye.
- *Cascadia* – A rooftop journey on the buildings of Las Palmas de Gran Canaria.

As you can see, they're pretty varied. Oh, and for what it's worth, my studies have shown that an interesting theme can increase a viral's 'watchability' by exactly 47.62 per cent.

The Riding

For me, the riding is *everything*, but it's usually the second component I consider while planning a new video. After I've settled on a theme, I tend to think, What new tricks do I fancy landing? I'll write down a list of what might be within my capabilities, plus any stuff known not to have been previously filmed on a trials bike. All the lines have to be of the highest possible standard. They also have to fit within the theme I've set for myself. A perfect example is when I did a bunny-hop front flip on to an exercise ball in *Imaginate*.

That idea came about during the rehab for my back injury. I had been using an exercise ball to strengthen my back. I had also been planning the props I'd imagined finding in my childhood bedroom. On my list were tennis and rubber balls, so it wasn't long before the two ideas came together.

Hmm, was I able to use the exercise ball during a stunt?

I thought. I then worked out that I could do a bunny-hop front flip, landing on the ball, back first, and using its spring to bounce me up again, so I'd get both wheels back on to the ground. After getting the trick down in the Kelvin Hall, I upped the ante by landing on the railway tracks at our replica railway station. I hadn't seen that done on a bike before, let alone in a video.

Location

It didn't take me long to realize that location was super-important in the making of an internet viral. It's where I tie my theme and tricks together, but a video is only as good as the stuff a rider utilizes – the obstacles, street furniture and lines. If you're shooting outdoors, it's important to find interesting objects to ride on, but they have to be in interesting locations. A phone box is great, but a phone box positioned in front of rolling hills and a setting sun in the Lake District is even better. That's when the time you invest in good scouting can really pay off.

But not every line has to be in place already. Think about this for a second: most of the lines I've filmed up to this point could have been built in a studio. The front flip in *Way Back Home* could have been done in a boring warehouse; likewise, the spiky fence in *Inspired Bicycles*. Instead, we found those lines in city locations, which is what captured so much attention. Even when we made *Imagine* in a warehouse-style space, our set was designed in such a way that it didn't look like the shell of Glasgow's Museum of Transport. Effectively, the viewer was peeking into the bedroom of my younger self, rather than into a huge building awaiting redevelopment.

The Hook

I like my videos to start with some atmospheric scene-setting. It's usually a shot or two of me cycling around, though in *The Ridge* I rowed towards the Skye shoreline in a boat. These images are designed to establish what I'm doing and where I'm doing it. Some epic music also helps to set the tone.

After that, the hook: a trick to grip the viewer right out of the gate. Take the front flip off the battlements at Edinburgh Castle in *Way Back Home* or that bloody spiky fence during *Inspired Bicycles*. The hook has shock value; it creates a buzz and sets a high standard for the rest of the action. People can turn off very quickly when they're watching stuff online, so I use the hook to engage them emotionally through fear, surprise or humour.

I also like the music to kick in around the hook. It could be a lyric that's somehow linked to what I'm doing in a shot, or the beginning of a heavy chorus, but it has to have *impact*. When we featured 'The Funeral' by Band of Horses on *Inspired Bicycles*, the song's slow-burning intro was timed to soundtrack my struggle on the spiky fence. Starting with a single vocal and a gentle guitar part, Dave edited the footage so the bass, drums and guitars kicked in as I dropped to the ground, having negotiated the railings. The next scene was a tyre-tap off a tree in the Meadows. You can hear the guitars surging; the drums are pounding. Hopefully, by this point, everybody watching has been drawn in.

Film Direction and Editing

These two go hand in hand, and I've been incredibly lucky with the dudes I've worked with so far. Some of them were initially mates from the Edinburgh bike scene and have gone on to become talented directors and editors, like Stu Thomson. Others, such as Dave Sowerby, were well respected before we began working together. Those guys both edit and direct their videos, which is important, because the final cuts don't become disconnected from the original theme that way; they see the project through from start to finish – hook to banger. Continuity is key.

A good riding director is vital – somebody who can expertly capture the riding in a way that reveals how hard the lines are, and the scale of the jumps and tricks. Everything I do has to be framed with the overall concept in mind. So, in *The Ridge*, Stu featured cutaway shots of the Black Cuillins range and one of the area's inhabitants – a seal that followed us as we rowed towards the shoreline. In *Inspired Bicycles*, Dave wanted to set everything within Edinburgh, so he filmed the city architecture and buildings as 'filler'.

By capturing plenty of extra material, as well as any potential difficulties in a trick, or scenes showing run-ups, the editing process becomes much easier. There are extra clips to play with – stuff that can set the mood or add to the drama of the stunts. As for editing, the story and tricks are always explained through music. The timing of the riding to the chosen soundtrack is a priority of editing; done well, it can seem as if the two are working in tandem. Watch a great BMX or skateboard film: the rider will often take off or land on a cymbal crash or a drumbeat.

What works for me (not in all projects, but in most of them) is a track with a slow-building intro. When the music is quiet at the beginning, it's easier to reveal scene-setting shots, stuff that establishes the theme, like the aforementioned seal. From there, everything should ramp up around the time of the hook, with a couple of smaller tricks thrown in.

I like to work with a track that has peaks and troughs – quiet to loud, or slow to fast – so I can weave in the various styles of riding we've filmed. Some stunts are one-hit wonders; others are longer lines that incorporate several shots; if you're super-advanced, some tricks might even require a drone camera. The right soundtrack will allow all of these to fit together without jarring. And, ideally, try to find a song that finishes on a high, or at least has a point of crescendo. That way, you can create an even more dramatic ending through the editing.

The Tunes

Music is a bit of an obsession of mine when it comes to putting together a viral. From my time cutting about Dunvegan,

Edinburgh and Glasgow, I've learned that listening to tunes can alter my interpretation of the spaces around me. The right music can also shift the dramatic feel of a film. Whenever I plan a shoot, I'm certain of what kind of lines I want to do and what kind of mood I want to bring to the visuals. So, for weeks, I'll skip through Spotify, searching for the perfect track, one that matches my ideas for atmosphere.

I'm realistic: I've given up on using the likes of Fleetwood Mac or Bon Jovi. Instead, I search for bands that are off the radar, or look like they might blow up in the near future. So when we used Ben Howard's track 'The Wolves' for *Industrial Revolutions*, he was on the verge of breaking. Just by luck, his career hit the mainstream shortly afterwards.

With *Imaginate*, it was a different set-up. When I was a kid, I watched a lot of eighties cartoons like *Teenage Mutant Ninja Turtles*, *Mask* and *Transformers*. Those shows always featured epic-sounding theme tunes. Sometimes they even bordered on hair metal. I wanted to capture a feeling of nostalgia. Stu found the track 'Runaway' by the Swedish rock band Houston and, with their big guitars and catchy synths, they gave *Imaginate* its eighties vibe.

When I watch certain action-sports films, I can get a bit critical of the music. The shots I'm seeing might be amazing, but if a director has put a clichéd sports theme over the top it undoes a lot of the effort. It's hard for big companies to license tracks from bands (it costs a fortune), but if people were a little bit more adventurous with the artists they used it would make all the difference. My advice? Get on to Spotify and explore.

The Banger

The big finish. An ender. The climax. Often a one-hit trick that pushes a rider to their limits, or a spectacular stunt like Ruben Alcantara's closing part in *Grounded*. For his grand finale, Ruben started by pedalling flat out along a freeway, before carving into a car park and up the side of a pillar supporting a pedestrian walkway (while gapping over *another* walkway in the process). His wallride took him thirty feet up in the air. When Ruben landed, he rode straight back on to the freeway. It was mind-blowing. Or, from the outside looking in: *madness*.

The banger concept came from BMX and skateboarding videos, and it has to be something that defies belief. So, for example, it adds some drama if a jump feels technically difficult, unbelievable in size or carries the threat of serious injury. One such trick happened as we were finishing *The Ridge*. There was a final line I was keen to go at, a bump front flip over a barbed-wire fence by one of the island's camp sites. It needed me to hit the wire with my front tyre, flip over and land on to a grassy bank. The incline led down to a sandy beach, which would have created a natural ending to the film: to anyone watching, it was as if I'd gone from one cove of the island to another. It was also the perfect chance to end with a banger.

I had done some full-on riding over those past few days, up and down the Black Cuillins, so the barbed-wire fence didn't seem like too much of a mental hurdle, but it was still a little scary. I knew that if I hit the fence too hard, my bike and I would part company – it would have been impossible to hold on to the handlebars. Too soft, and I wouldn't have been able to generate the momentum needed to get myself over the wire. To practise, we borrowed some crash mats from a nearby school and strengthened the fence. I spent an hour getting it right. At first, the fence was too solid and the impact forced the bike to catapult out of my hands. On other occasions, I managed to bring myself around, only to land on my back or side. I lost count of the aborted run-ups deleted by Stu that day.

There was also the barbed wire to take into account. One wrong move and I'd be in ribbons, which wouldn't have been pretty. But that element of extra danger created the perfect mood for a banger. The trick also had a relatable quality. Everybody knew how tall a barbed-wire fence could be; a lot of people would have climbed over one at some point, or might have carried their bicycle over the top. They had a feeling for what I was doing and the risks I was taking. Plus, I was using my Santa Cruz mountain bike rather than the Inspired, which upped the difficulty of the riding. When I finally managed to hurl myself across, landing two wheels on the bank before cycling down to the beach, I knew the banger was in the bag and my formula was complete.

One thing, though: please, please, *please*, just be careful, would you? I am all for inspiring a new riding video, but I don't want to be held responsible for your hospital visits.

Oh, and something else: if you're not scared while doing a banger, you're either a) mad or b) not trying hard enough.

Scene Twenty-one

FADE IN

(EXT.) The River Thames

Danny stands at the top of a huge ramp that has been positioned on a floating barge. At the bottom is his next trick: a huge loop-the-loop. The city lights are reflecting in the water. A large crowd has gathered on the embankment. Danny is psyching himself up. It's as if he's thinking, how the heck did I get here? As he looks down at the drop, we can see him putting his headphones on. He's nodding to the beat of the music — it's 'New York Groove' by the American rock band Kiss.

He drops off the edge and races towards the loop . . .

Danny MacAskill, Make It Happen —
The Loop, 2014

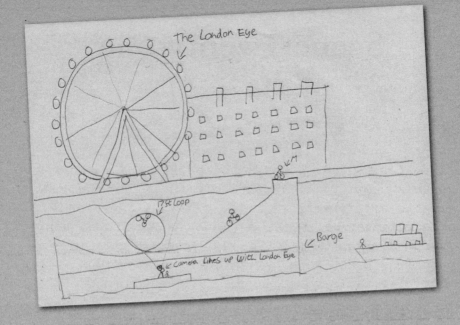

21. Musical Interlude

Music has been a constant in my life. It inspires me to go out in the wind and the rain. As a kid, I wasn't thinking in terms of video ideas or dramatic story arcs. I was focused on learning new tricks and imagining the ways in which I could jump from different obstacles. By the time I was fifteen I'd started my ritual of riding alone. My friends lived over five miles away, and music became a nice substitute for not always having someone to talk to as I hit the Gun Shop, so I'd borrow Mum's Walkman and listen to albums like *Play* by Moby. I loved stuff that created an epic vibe as I tried to do 180s and 360s. I enjoyed discovering new bands and often I'd make mix tapes. The album *Sunday 8PM* by techno group Faithless became one of my soundtracks during the winter of 1999. Songs like their hit single 'God is a DJ' kept me motivated as I was cutting around under the streetlights in the pouring rain.

Music quickly became so much more than a way of killing the silence. It took my riding to a different place. By soundtracking those hours on the bike, I discovered different perspectives on familiar challenges. Old obstacles felt fresh if I was playing a new track. I might have hopped from the same slab of concrete a hundred times, but with 'Porcelain' by Moby in my head, I'd view the environment in a new way. My approach speeds would change with the rhythm. Different moods would inspire me to try different lines. Through my headphones, a limited riding terrain in Dunvegan was given fresh perspective.

At a talk I gave at the Edinburgh Science Festival with Professor Ian Robertson, I was told that all top sportspeople are great psychologists, masters of controlling their own mind.

'Some people get very jaded with life,' he said. 'They get bored that things are the same, but here we have you, in the same objective situation, where you're saying, "Oh, I've done this trick a thousand times, it's boring!" But you keep it constantly fresh by using music to change the context. That's of incredible importance, because novelty grows our brains by stimulating a drug called noradrenaline . . .'

That might have been an important element in how I got to where I am today. Noradrenaline helps to increase a person's focus. Like adrenaline, it can also mobilize the body for action. Listening to music on my bike as a kid, I could reimagine my surroundings. The weather might have been shocking, but a tape of tunes and the Rider's Eye gave me the motivation to enjoy the elements. With a little imagination, my world felt very different from behind those handlebars.

Music also drives my ideas. And whenever it comes to focusing on a jump, or overcoming a mental hurdle like the five of diamonds in *Imaginate*, I can spend hours listening to the same tracks to tune myself in, or overcome the jitters. Music also drives my ideas. And whenever it comes to focusing on a jump, or overcoming a mental hurdle like the five of diamonds in *Imaginate*, I can spend hours listening to the same tracks to tune myself in, or overcome the jitters. In *Imaginate* I used Tame Impala's 'Elephant'.

That's when I use my headphones. For some of the bangers I've done in the past, I tend to play the same song on repeat. In *Imaginate* I used Tame Impala's 'Elephant'. 'New York Groove' by Kiss helped me through a loop-the-loop I rode over the River Thames for an advert. If ever I'm having a hard time getting myself to the point of no return, I'll play a tune that will push me over the edge. When it gets to the chorus or a part of the verse that I like, I use it as a mental cue. It tells me to 'Go!'

I talk to myself a lot in those moments, too. Some of the stunts I've completed are by far the biggest challenges I have ever faced in my life, and in my head I'm often thinking, You know you can do this, but . . . *what if?* I understand I'm perfectly capable of executing whatever it is I've decided to do, but the more cautious part of my brain won't allow me to go there without a fight.

To get over the fear, I tell myself that it's going to be fine: that I can do it, no problem. Sometimes, I use headphones to shut out external noise like traffic, which can affect me if

I'm trying to concentrate, especially if a line might have serious consequences. It can be difficult to feel mentally primed, even more so if there's a crowd of pedestrians nearby and the police might come along. Even the wind can put me on edge sometimes.

There are periods where I can't push through this barrier, especially if I've been riding for days, or weeks, in the build-up and I'm tired, mentally and physically. That might have been the reason for my struggle with the tyre-tap front flip off the battlements at Edinburgh Castle. I *wanted* to do the trick. I *knew* I could do the trick. But my brain had other ideas. It said: Are you sure you want to flip off this wall?

It was because I was working in the unknown. I had only done that jump on to our crash mats twenty minutes before, and even then I'd barely managed a 50 per cent success rate. Once the mats were removed, one part of my brain filled with fear and self-doubt. The other fought back. I imagined how I would feel if I was lying in bed the next day, having *not* gone through with it. I've always said that injuring myself while committing to an idea is far better than being fully fit, having not tried. I can't live with regret.

When I've watched other riders during the making of their videos, especially in BMX or mountain biking, and I've seen their polished product, I don't imagine them going through the same crazy anguish as me. Other bikers seem to have more control over their mental state – not all, but some. They're calm and they're calculated. They can reach their goals, no problem.

I guess genes and mental hardwiring come into play with

those guys. It might also depend on how they've grown up: if someone learned their tricks in a gang of mates, like a lot of kids did, they might possess a bit more drive. The competitive edge instilled in them by their friends might be enough to get them to commit more readily. I grew up riding alone a lot of the time. It's probably why I don't carry the same reckless streak. I also always know I can physically execute whatever I've planned. Like a lot of extreme-sports folk, I have my limits. I understand what I'm capable of at the top end of my ability, and I'm aware of what can go on in that 'zone'.

Still, nailing something new means I have to endure all sorts of anxiety. With my headphones on, I can shut it all out. I can make that leap into the unknown.

While we're talking about music, it's a good time to look at some of the artists who have delivered the soundtracks to my films. It's important to recognize the bands that I've used: it's a respect thing. After all, if somebody took chunks of my footage without asking, I'd be a bit annoyed. So here, then, are the bands that have played a part so far . . .

Inspired Bicycles

'The Funeral', Band of Horses (*Everything all the Time*, 2006)

For our first video, Dave and I wanted a song that captured the epic mood: something that matched the ambition of

Ruben Alcantara's *Grounded*. There were plenty of bands on the shortlist, and our first choice was 'Hoppípolla', a track by the Icelandic post-rock band Sigur Rós. But just as we prepared our early edits, the BBC released a trailer for their new David Attenborough show, *Planet Earth*.

I couldn't believe it! The producers had used the same song, and their imagery was incredible. Snow leopards stalked their prey in the mountains. There was also a slo-mo shot of a great white shark clamping its bloody gnashers around a helpless seal. Everybody was talking about the advert, and that meant they were also talking about the music, so we were forced to change our plans. Luckily, 'The Funeral' was just as epic.

I'd love to meet Band of Horses one day. It's funny: I feel like we've become a part of one another; their music is such an important part of *Inspired Bicycles*, and I suppose that makes them a big part of my life: their music soundtracked where my professional riding career started.

Way Back Home

'Wax and Wire', Loch Lomond (*Night Bats* EP, 2009)
'A Little Piece', The Jezabels (*Dark Storm* EP, 2010)

We stumbled across both Loch Lomond and The Jezabels while driving around Scotland in the mobile home. Loch Lomond were a Portland indie band, while The Jezabels were from Sydney. As we criss-crossed the countryside, my disco ball spinning in the back, Loch Lomond blared out of the sub woofers, and they became an anthem for our road trip.

Industrial Revolutions

'The Wolves', Ben Howard (*Every Kingdom*, 2011)

We were in a race against time to get this track included in the video. Stu had picked it up from his friend at Universal; Ben Howard was an English singer-songwriter who was under the radar. I was pleased that we'd got the track but, one day, as I was driving up the M8 to Dumbarton, 'The Wolves' came on the radio. It was being played by DJ Zane Lowe, who described it as 'our hottest new record in the world today!'

I immediately freaked out that it might be taken from us. I also worried that it might suffer from overkill by the time the *Concrete Circus* documentary came out on Channel 4. I didn't want the song to get super-popular. 'The Wolves' didn't go as stratospheric and by the time the clip was released, it didn't feel overplayed. Good news for both of us.

Imaginate

'Runaway', Houston (*Relaunch*, 2011)

Imaginate was all about nostalgia. We needed a song that matched the mood. As I've said previously, Houston are a Swedish rock band with an eighties vibe – they reminded me of some of the hair-metal bands like Europe from back in the day – and when I thought back to what was playing on the radio when I was a kid, that's what sprung to mind. Their sound added a little extra atmosphere to what I was doing.

Epecuén

'Night Wolves', Farewell J.R (*Health*, 2013)
'Long Highway', The Jezabels (*Prisoner*, 2011)

I drove myself mad getting the music sorted for *Epecuén*. Because it was such an emotive film, I was desperate to get it just right. Every day, I would search for powerful songs that might suit the mood of devastation within the town. By the time I'd finished shooting I had several hundred tracks on a playlist. Whenever I was on a plane or sitting at home, I would stare at a screen grab from the shoot, listening to different songs and trying to figure out the right one.

The trickiest part was finding something that suited our long, sweeping drone shots over the crumbling city. The music needed to match the end-of-days mood and eventually, we opted for another track by The Jezabels, plus a new discovery, Farewell J.R. Dave and I still had a few arguments about what should be included, I reckon because I'd been thinking about it for so long. We were also getting a bit of interference from Red Bull on some of the songs that we had wanted to include – I think they felt some of our choices were too emotive, which caused a few tantrums at our end. We only ever want the best for our work: that's why we do everything within our power to find the perfect soundtrack. In the end, both the track by The Jezabels and Farewell J.R seemed to match those dramatic scenes of destruction.

The Ridge

'Blackbird', Martyn Bennett (*Grit*, 2003)

Martyn Bennett was a Canadian artist who mixed traditional Celtic music with breaks and beats. The first time I ever heard him was one night in Epecuén. The daylight was fading and the area always had these amazing sunsets; everything turned blood-red, and flocks of flamingos would fly overhead as the crew gathered around for a barbecue.

I was lying out on a crash mat when my friend John first played 'Blackbird'; I chucked it on to my Cuillins playlist, thinking it had the right sound for a film I was planning to make with Stu later in the year. I knew we had to go down the traditionally Scottish route, without being too cheesy. I didn't want to be standing at the top of the Inaccessible Pinnacle playing a set of bagpipes in my kilt, but 'Blackbird' seemed to strike the right balance.

It wasn't until we had committed to using it and were adding our clips to the music that I learned Martyn had died in 2005. I was shocked on hearing the news. I hope *The Ridge* delivered a fitting platform for his work.

Scene Twenty-two

<u>FADE IN</u>

(<u>INT.</u>) A rooftop apartment in Las Palmas de
Gran Canaria

Danny grabs his bike and helmet, which has been
fixed with a POV camera, and heads for the door.
We cut to a portable radio. The DJ is giving a
weather forecast.

(<u>EXT.</u>) The rooftops of Las Palmas

A drone camera captures the Las Palmas horizon;
there are a series of flat rooftops painted in
vibrant colours — yellows, reds, oranges, blues
and greens.

The next time we see Danny, he is riding along a
wall that separates two buildings. Either side
of him is an exposed drop of at least two
storeys. A fall here would have very serious
consequences . . .

                              Cascadia, 2015

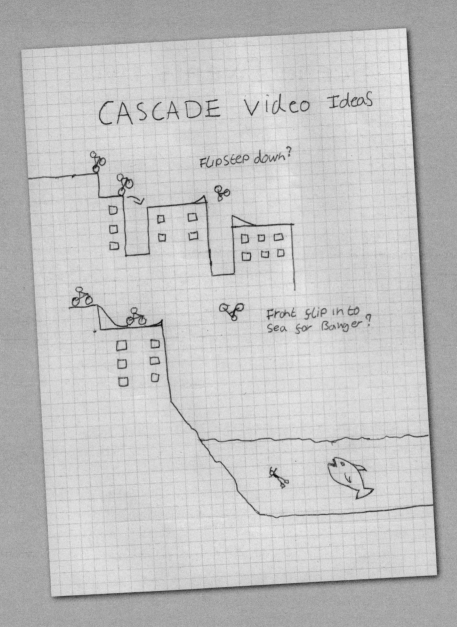

22. It's a Long Way Down

The thought of riding across a series of rooftops had excited me for ages and, once I'd finished *The Ridge*, I began flicking through my notebook and noticed the idea scribbled down. It fired me up. I knew the technology we'd used during the making of our last couple of virals – particularly the drone camera brought in by Stu and his brother-in-law Lec on the Black Cuillins Mountains – meant that my riding could be captured from the air. The drone racing over the brightly coloured buildings, the camera hovering above me as I manualled past satellite dishes and hanging laundry, would be the canvas for my new video idea.

I was due to make a video with GoPro and I figured that if I attached one to my helmet it would make for a great point-of-view film. Anyone watching would get a sense for the exposed drops and roads below me and, when I suggested the plan, GoPro were up for it. It wasn't long before I was scouring the internet for suitable locations. At first, a place I'd found in Mexico seemed ideal, but when somebody mentioned Las Palmas de Gran Canaria, my attention shifted. The buildings were exactly as I'd envisioned when I was first struck by the idea. Painted in vivid shades of yellow, red, blue and orange, they cascaded down a hill, which led to a cliff and the Atlantic Ocean.

This time around, I wanted to bring in Robbie Meade as my director. He had worked with Stu on *Imaginate* and had acted as our second camera operator during the production of *Epecuén*. The pair of us had built up a strong relationship over the past few years, and Robbie was world-class when it came to operating a MOVI (that's shorthand for a gyro-stabilized camera gimbal).

Once we had arrived in Las Palmas with a local 'fixer' called Ian, Robbie and I began establishing where to shoot and what roofs to ride. However, it was impossible to make a decision on locations without actually standing above the city. Three of the boys from my awesome team of friends had to start knocking on doors in San Juan, one of the poorer neighbourhoods, and ask for permission to investigate the rooftops. It was an interesting process. Firstly, Ian would make his introductions, and usually what followed was a heated conversation with plenty of arm-waving thrown in. It nearly always got fiery but, as I soon discovered, this was a common negotiating technique and, more often than not, we were allowed to nose around. Usually, a coffee, or something a bit stronger, was offered along the way. I couldn't work out whether Ian was one of the most charming folk in Gran Canaria or the head of a local mafia organization.

We must have investigated at least forty rooftops, and I grew in confidence as I assessed the distances between each building, even though a lot of the routes came with high-risk consequences; I listed a string of lines that took me along ledges and walls where one slip could have sent me tumbling seventy-odd feet to the streets below. With each suggestion, Robbie would look at me as if to say: OK, if you're calling out that flip over an alleyway then we're doing it . . . There were plenty of raised eyebrows.

Sure enough, when it actually came to riding, my attitude altered a little. It's one thing to say you're going to land a hop from one ledge to another with an exposed drop to one side. It's an altogether different experience doing it. And once we'd started shooting, my body felt a little stiff for the first few shots, probably because I knew I'd have to keep my wits about me. But I also knew that I couldn't allow for any serious fear to creep in. Getting scared often causes the brain and body to make silly mistakes, and I had no room for error.

There were security measures in place, though. I'd cycled across enough ledges to know how to correct myself if ever I thought I was heading for trouble. Whenever I gapped to a ledge or hopped up to a balcony, I'd weight myself ever so slightly to one side. That way, my balance could be tipped towards the building if necessary, rather than towards any exposed fall. My balance distribution meant that I could manoeuvre to the 'safe' side of the wall (by 'safe' I mean the smaller fall out of my two options, and sometimes there are simply no favourable options – in which case, mistakes are just out of the question).

To keep myself calm, I imagined each balcony or railing was a flowerbed at the Gun Shop or a wall in Glasgow. The dimensions of the surfaces were identical; the consequences of falling were very different. If I had been edging my way along a two-foot-wide wall at home, I wouldn't have fretted. The only difference here was the daunting exposure to one side, rather than a row of neatly pruned roses.

I thought, I don't want to fall down there. But if I do, I should probably aim for the soft-top convertible . . .

There was one unexpected challenge. The sun, which I'd craved while making *Way Back Home* and *Inspired Bicycles*, was proving to be a royal pain in the arse. At first, when I started riding Las Palmas, I felt a little tense, but I couldn't figure out why. I seemed unable to gauge my distances accurately, and that made me nervous. It was only once a cloud had passed overhead and the light dropped slightly that I got a handle on the problem. Because a lot of the buildings were white, the sun would bounce back off the paintwork, creating a dazzling glare. The bright light was affecting my vision.

I decided to suck it up. Sunglasses weren't an option because they would have messed with the continuity of the film. I could hardly wear a pair of shades in one scene but not in another – I don't think it would have looked right anyway. Instead, I put the sun to the back of my mind, along with any doubts regarding mechanical reliability and a fall of several storeys to the traffic. It was time to get on with it.

We started at the top of Las Palmas and worked our way to the cliffs. The story in our heads comprised a dramatic cycle route from the hills of San Juan to the sea at El Roque. The title was *Cascadia*, and we began with a clip of me leaving a top-floor apartment, the radio playing, before grabbing my bike and riding out to the roof. From there, I descended through the city, cruising along ledges, gapping to balconies and manualling along walls. The opening shots suggested I was just another cyclist on his way to the office or beach. The rest of the video, however, presented *Cascadia* as something different to that . . . a little more risky, let's say.

As always, we scooped up the easiest tricks first. I rode the rooftops solidly for three days, but at the back of my mind was the first of two bangers I had to complete: a front flip off a cliff at El Roque which took me into the sea. The drop was around fifty feet, but it could have been so much bigger. We had initially considered a jumping-off point where the fall was more like ninety feet in height, but when one of the production team (a trained diver and surf photographer) explored the landing area, he discovered the water was only fifteen feet deep, which wrote off the prospect of doing the bigger drop.

In the end, we settled on El Roque. At the top of the cliff

was an alleyway between two buildings that overlooked the water. Building work had been taking place on the road, and we convinced the scaffolding team to let us construct a short tower in the street. With the help of George and John, we built a series of platforms so that I could drop from the rooftops on to a ramp before racing towards the cliff edge and tipping off into the unknown. From there, I had to sail for a little while, picking my landing spot in the water like an Olympic diver, prior to tucking in, rotating and splashing down.

On paper, it was quite straightforward and wouldn't need any advanced riding technique. The jump was so simple I even worried what the riding scene would make of it. I mean, who does an ender into water? But the dangers were all too apparent as I looked over the edge. Whenever the tide rolled in, the water foamed ominously. I could see myself being pulled all over the place by the current. The view became even worse once the water had been sucked out – that's when a series of jagged rocks was revealed. If I was to overshoot them, I needed to gather a fair bit of speed. I knew that, with enough momentum, my chances of injury were minimal. I had belly-flopped from the falls of Falloch (off Loch Lomond, Scotland) earlier that year. The drop had been around forty feet and, while the blow of landing in the water wasn't pleasant, it hadn't injured me. I figured, If I can survive that, this should be no different. But just for precautionary reasons, I padded my underwear with some cycling shorts.

The El Roque cliff became a real mind-twister. At first, I was fine. My confidence was high. I'd been riding well for a few days. I figured a run-up or two would be enough to get myself geared up to jump, but that all changed when I first dropped off the scaffolding and pedalled towards the water. I worried that I might not gather the speed needed to clear the rocks, and every time I approached the ramp's lip I would slam on the brakes. All I could think was, I'm only going to clear those rocks by a few feet – *at best*.

Like with so many of my tricks, the passing minutes quickly turned into an hour; the voices of doubt in my head were chattering away and, as the sun dipped below the horizon, I could sense our chances of completing the banger slipping away. The scaffolding was being taken down in the morning and there was another big line cued up for the next day – a back flip over an alley between two school rooftops – but that was taking place at the top of the hill. For the climax of our film to match the storyline (and make any sense), I had to finish in the sea. I was a little stressed – perhaps the most anxious I'd felt since *Imaginate*. George, who was hanging under the scaffolding in a harness, looking like a construction worker, gave me some stern words of reassurance, which helped a little, but I could tell that the locals who had gathered to watch me were probably now considering me to be a bit of a wimp. They had been peering out of their windows to catch the action and were now pretty bored of the wait.

I could feel myself getting into a bit of a rage, and that's when I dropped the nose, rattled down the shaking scaffolding and threw myself off the edge.

There was no rush of fear, no sick, lurching sensation, just that familiar feeling of sheer bloody relief. As I tucked into the front flip, all I could hear was the swishing of my wheels and the sound of the wind battering my ears. When I rotated, I opened out, expecting to hit the sea, but soon realized that I had another fifteen-foot fall to the ocean. The sea was rushing up towards me; the sky was turning over above. I could hear a faint cheering coming from the locals on the cliff. I kept a firm grip on my handlebars as if I was landing an ordinary jump, and my front wheel broke the water first, saving me from a nasty slap in the face. Only a few seconds had passed since leaving the clifftop. Now I was submerged. Foam, bubbles and bike washed around me as I broke through the surface, gasping for air.

It was such a great feeling, but as I raised my arm triumphantly, I was engulfed by a huge wave and, almost like a stalemate situation, I was being held in place as the riptide cancelled out the waves towards shore. It was probably more dangerous than the drop I had just done. Because I was still in my jeans, I felt weighed down and, once I'd recovered from the shock, it took me twenty minutes to make my way to the beach. At one point, my helmet was ripped off in the swell, which caused a surge of panic because my GoPro was fixed to the top – *the one with all the footage on it!* When I saw it bobbing to the surface, I was able to make a grab for the chin strap. What a relief. Losing the spoils of our work would not have been an option. And I wouldn't have heard the end of it.

Back-flipping over an alley between two schools isn't something I do every day – I'm not a freerider, after all. But the jump was Robbie's hook for *Cascadia* and, despite the heart-swooping sensation of flying across a three-storey-high drop, I knew the line would be worthwhile. Our film was going to look great, and I trusted everybody around me to make it succeed. George and John had built the ramps; there were airbags for my practice run-ups, and the GoPro had been set to capture the POV footage. Meanwhile, a drone buzzed overhead, its flight path following a road bordered with palm trees. The wind had dropped; out came the sun. I made a promise that I wasn't going to repeat the trauma of the previous day.

This time, I said to myself, I'm taking five practice run-ups and then I'm going at it – whatever.

Of course, it didn't pan out that way. While the trick was fairly basic – I was launching myself off one ramp and flying a distance of twenty feet while back-flipping, before landing on another ramp on the opposite building – several outside factors had unsettled me. For starters, there was the run-up to take into consideration. Pulling out at the last minute would be a major issue and, if I bottled it, I'd have to slam on my brakes with plenty of distance to spare. Changing my mind with twenty feet to go, or less, would result in me skidding over the edge of a three-storey drop. As with most tricks, it is far more dangerous to lose your head than just commit to the line. In no time at all, five practice runs became twenty. I was getting wound up.

Come on, I've got this, I told myself. I can hit that ramp, I can do the flip easily. And once I'm on the other side, I need never do it again . . .

But the more I thought about it, the more anxiety clouded my ambition. I could see the drone. It had been in the sky for ages and I worried the team would have to bring it down for recharging. Was the battery in my camera also going to die on me? I soon sensed that everybody was thinking the same thing, which made matters even worse. So I reverted to what had become my go-to psychological reboot: I put my headphones on and took myself away for a wee while.

Long before Robbie and I had arrived in Gran Canaria, our music for *Cascadia* had been in place. 'Fools', a track by American indie band The Dodos, had seemed to fit our concept perfectly – it had a pounding drumbeat. As with *Industrial Revolutions*, I'd use the song to cue various stunts as I was riding. I would put my phone down on the floor and play 'Fools' through its speakers, pushing at the pedals on a certain note or lyric, committing to a line across a ledge, or gapping from one rooftop to another.

There was a key moment in 'Fools' that I knew would soundtrack my flip across the 'school gap'. It arrived in the opening chorus with a lyric – 'And we don't do a thing, 'cause we're busy and think/ Just wandering, just a-wandering like fools . . .' Immediately afterwards, the backing vocals kicked in – '*Wo-oh! Wo-oh!*' – and it became a trigger; in that moment, I stuck both feet on the pedals and, as the song built up, I cranked towards the take-off, gathering momentum until my window of uncertainty had whizzed past – *I was going through with it.*

I fired off the ramp and looked backwards. The sky tumbled above me as my landing came into view. Instinctively, I realized I was over-rotating and that the landing was going to be heavy, though it wasn't enough to cause a problem. Shock waves pounded my wrists, but I was able to hold on. I'd made it. The stress and worry of Las Palmas was over and, as George jumped on my back in the excitement, our rooftop movie was in the bag.

In any other setting, my cutting about the balconies of San Juan or flipping off the cliff at El Roque would have probably seen me arrested. But with a legit production crew in support, I was able to push the riding as far as my creative vision would allow. I guess that was my riding life in a nutshell. *Cascadia* had been a fun video to make, if a little stressful at times, but I hadn't gone any bigger than my tricks on *Imaginate* or during *Way Back Home*. The concept had been ambitious, but the beauty of what I'd achieved was making the most of my ability to ride pretty much wherever I wanted. There was nobody in the city to kick me off my bike because I'd been given permission, and that had come about because of the team of friends I was working with. Funnily enough, one of the people who had initially objected to my riding across their roof was a local policeman. The drop from his building was about seventy feet, and the landing zone was a huge pile of rubble. He probably didn't want his apartment to be associated with anything unpleasant, but even he relented in the end.

That hadn't always been the case in the past. PC Duncan Carmichael hated me skidding about the Dunvegan streets at night. Even in Edinburgh and Glasgow I had to be wary of anyone who might object to my riding lines on their property. But with a camera crew and a decent idea, I could pick a location and work within it. From what I could tell, the only limitations to my riding were lack of imagination and confidence. With those in place, I could go just about anywhere.

Scene Twenty-three

<u>FADE IN</u>

(<u>INT.</u>) The Glasgow Transport Museum

It's one of the final scenes to be filmed for Imaginate. A portion of the studio has been built to resemble Danny's bedroom, this time in 'normal size'.

VOICEOVER: Elsewhere in Kelvin Hall, attention has turned to shooting the rest of the film. Here, on a human-sized replica of the giant set, a young Danny MacAskill will begin the journey into Danny's imagination.

The camera cuts to producer Mike Christie.

MIKE: What we've built is young Danny's bedroom, where young Danny's imagination has begun to run riot with all these amazing stunts and all these strange toys . . .

Danny's mum, Anne, has been roped in for a cameo in the video. She awaits her scene.

ANNE: My big moment, yes!

Moments later, she bursts into the bedroom to confront the actor portraying young Danny.

ANNE: Daniel, I'm going to shoot the boots off you if you don't stop mucking about on your bike and come and get your tea!'

MacAskill's Imaginate, Episode 5, 2013

THE ENDER

Hippy Hop Knee Slide

Double Flair

Barrel Roll over Ball

Playing Cards

23. Reinventing the Wheelie

What does your mum make of all this?

That's something a lot of people have asked me, usually after seeing *Cascadia* or *The Ridge*. It's something I think about a lot, as do a lot of folk who ride to extremes. I was watching a Red Bull documentary on Robbie Maddison recently, and he was talking about the same thing. Robbie's probably one of my biggest heroes in riding, even though he works with an engine rather than a trials bike. Like me, his passion for stunt biking had impacted on the people in his life.

Robbie's on another level, though. One of his jumps took him to the top of the replica Arc de Triomphe in Las Vegas – a height of a hundred feet. Had he flipped out or lost control, the fall would have killed him. After the jump, the cameras cut to a close-up of his wife, who was stressing out. The couple have two young kids together, so it was interesting to hear Robbie's take on risk and the consequences of what he does for a career.

'I got to a point there where everybody around me has said, "You're gonna kill yourself, you're crazy,"' he said. 'And I was like, "You guys don't understand." It's tough on Amy. She goes in and watches, and I know she freaks out when I jump. She says all kinds of crazy stuff, but she's there watching . . . It's a whole way of living.

'I have another big jump coming up, and Amy's terrified about it. She's not living the dream going to these events, she's living *my* dream and I'm putting her through hell . . . I'm not doing this for money and recognition. I'm doing this because it's my dream. *This is what I do.*'

With his riding, Robbie is pushing his motorbike harder than anybody else and, like a lot of extreme bike riders, he's had his accidents. He's fractured his skull three times during different wipe-outs, and afterwards everyone says the same thing: *Imagine being his wife, she must go through a lot.* While I'm not married, people understandably make similar comments about my family. But, to be honest, my mum is cut from a different cloth; she doesn't seem to worry at all. When I started riding my bike professionally, she would buy bundles of newspapers every week, such as the *Scotsman* or the *Herald*. If ever I were mentioned, she would ring up, proud as anything. My dad is the same, though he can get a bit anxious. After I'd released *Inspired Bicycles*, he took me to one side.

'You might as well just leave it there, Daniel,' he said. 'Don't go out and hurt yourself . . .'

Mum hasn't gone that far and she's very realistic about what I get up to. She even had that cameo role in *Imaginate*. Now she has her own Internet Movie Database profile, and she's listed in the *Imaginate* credits as the actress who played 'Young Daniel's mum'.

My half-brothers and half-sisters can get a little stressed out. During the Edinburgh Science Fest, somebody asked me what my family thought of my work, which was when Muriel, who was also in the audience, piped up.

'I look at what Daniel does and it actually scares me,' she said. 'I can't bear to watch while he's filming. *Imaginate* was terrifying. I stood there, silent, in fear. I was there with [my kids] Tania and Thomas when the tank was in the building – and that wipe-out when he fell off the gun? I was on the phone to the ambulance service while Daniel was lying there, going, "Oh, what happened?" He did call me later to apologize for giving us such a big fright . . .'

As far as my extended family is concerned, my aunties just want to hear from me when the job is done. They avoid the stresses of hearing what I am attempting to do.

I've also had issues with making relationships work over the years, not because of the risks I'm taking but because I can become single-minded when I'm on a project. It consumes everything. I spend days, maybe weeks, just researching the music. Even more time is spent looking for locations, and that's before I've started riding. When I'm squeezing other commitments into that workload, like travelling and sponsorship meetings, maintaining a relationship can be tricky.

Some athletes can make their relationships work quite easily. Both partners are able to support one another; they can help each other out in every aspect of their lives. But I like to focus on my projects entirely and, when I'm not making films, I want to go out and ride. So, right now, I don't feel that I've got the space in my life for a relationship, but I'm more than happy about that. Girls I've been with in the past have been OK with the risks I'm taking. They know that I'm not prepared to die doing what I do, though it is better to die doing something that you love. It's just that I'm not prepared to allow restrictions to get in the way of my goals.

I released my first online viral in 2009 and, sometimes, I wonder whether my riding has improved at all. My concepts and ideas have become more ambitious but, when I first made *Inspired Bicycles* with Dave Sowerby in Edinburgh, I was a bloke working in a bicycle shop. I was fixated on riding, and only riding. Whenever I was away from my bike, working in Macdonald Cycles or at home in bed, I could feel my hunger growing for trials and tricks.

These days, it's different. The bike has become my business. I'm always travelling about, making videos, touring with Drop and Roll or taking on interesting challenges for sponsors and film-makers. That means I don't get as much time riding for myself as I used to. But don't get me wrong – it's cool, I love it, and sometimes I can't believe my luck. My only complaint is that I lose the opportunity to concentrate on the really important stuff – riding. It may not sound so important to you, but it is vital for me and I feel out of sorts if I don't save some time for myself.

I'm not the only one on the extreme-sports scene who worries that their creativity will plateau; from what I can tell, it's quite a common concern. The US freeclimber Alex Honnold is a bit like me. He reckons his style hasn't improved over the last couple of years, mainly because he's not had the time to learn anything new. That's why I've tried to take people into different places with my videos. During the making of *Way Back Home*, *Industrial Revolutions* and *The Ridge*, I used a lot of the skills I'd learned years previously, but I was updating them and weaving them together within a concept suited to that style. In the next couple of years, I want to take time to work on new techniques and ideas.

I'm not always going to be able to ride the bike like I do now – not when I'm in my forties or fifties. When I was a kid, I used to flick through the pages of *Mountain Biking UK* and see the ages of riders such as Martyn Ashton. Woah, I'd think. He's twenty-seven – *that's old*. Now I'm past that age, my attitude has changed. I still feel like a teenager, but there must be a reason why so many people quit riding in their mid- to late thirties. That's why I'm keen to do as much as I can in the next few years, before the bumps and the bruises take too much of a toll.

As I get older, I'll just have to think about riding a little differently. I'll have to adapt. Luckily, I can make a viral at any age, and I don't actually have to be the one doing the physical work. I'd like to try my hand at being a creative director. I want to take some of the experience I've gathered from my film-making and put it to work with someone else. Maybe I could make a viral video with an athlete at the top of their game? It could be another Red Bull name, like the US climber Sasha DiGiulian. Or an Olympic gold medallist might want to make a video that breaks the mould in their sport. (They're usually so focused on getting to the podium they rarely think about the creative possibilities that a film can open up for them.)

I also want to end my personal riding career with a bang. At some point, I'd love to work on a project similar to what Ruben Alcantara set out to achieve with *Grounded*: a part that highlighted his riding at the absolute max. It could be that I return to street trials or do something even more ambitious than *Imaginate* or *Cascadia*. But whatever it is, I have to make a stamp. That final video has to be a monumental achievement, just so I can give the new riders on the scene something to aim at. Because, whether I like it or not, my riding is going to be considered relatively tame at some stage in the future – that's just the way it goes. But it would be nice to know that I've inspired the internet generation in some way.

The good news is that, for now at least, the possibilities are limitless. Only the size of my ambitions, or injuries, can hold me back. The biggest problem is that there's too much fun to be had and not enough time to do it all in.

It looks like the race is on.

Take me to the next banger. *The ender.*

Acknowledgements

A lot of people have helped me to become the person I am today – both on and off my bike. My family has been incredibly important: Anne and Peter MacAskill – Mum and Dad – for giving me a reckless amount of freedom as a child; Margaret Ishbel MacAskill; Murial, Dave, Tanya and Thomas Prior; the MacAskills: Ewan, Gillian, Sarah, Tommy, Robin, Juliet and Laura; Mary, Rob, Peter and Katie Nelson; Margaret Hamilton, Jean and Sarah Hamilton (for keeping me rolling along on two wheels), and Peat Surfleet.

I couldn't have done it without my mates either – from Skye, Edinburgh, Glasgow – and others I've met along the way: Ricky Ingles, Andrew Cambel, Gordy Neill, Calum Matheson, Pat and Cambel Matheson, Jim and Carol Ingles, Donnie Macphie, Doreen and Angus Macphie, Jamie Stuart, Alex Kozikowski, Kenneth Mackinnon, Douglas Sutton, James Sutton, Ben Wear, Bill Edger, Alexander Lind and the Lind family, Graham Finney, Kevin Digman, and to all the other legends who make Skye the awesome place it is!

Then there are the friends I've made through riding: David Keegan, Martin Macbeth, Nash Masson, Mark MacIver,

Andy Toop, Colin Macdonald, Chaz Nairn, Fraser McNeil, Ian Hayes, Jay Castle, Sam Kennedy, John Bailey, George Eccleston, Forbes Howie, Dave Sowerby, Mark Huskisson, Andy McCandlish, Paul Smail, Alan Blyth, Fred Murray, Iain Withers, Kenny Wilson, Juliet Drummond, Stu Thomson, Amber Thomson, Davey Mackison, Duncan Shaw, Ben Travis, Ross Mcarthur, Fabio Wibmer, Myles Bonnar, Paul MacDonald, Herald Francis, and all the Macdonald Cycles folk I worked with over the years . . .

Then there's Taj Hendry, Robbie Meade, Aaron Bartlett, Darren Roberts, Henry Jackson, Iain Hayes, Ricky Crompton, Manu Uranga, James Thorne, Dr Bray, Garrett Bray, Brodie Mangan, Alastair Clarkson, Andrew MacLean, Michael Bonney, Martyn Ashton, The Athertons, Robin Kitchen, Pete Drew, Peter Clegg, Andrew Mee, Sebas Romero, Derek Brettell, Chris Akrigg, Hans (No Way) Rey, Jeff Lenosky, Ryan Leech, Martin Hayes, Martin Söderström, Andreu Lacondeguy, Mike Christie, *MBUK* magazine, Davey Cleaver, Jon Smith, Adam Read, TartyBikes, Lesley White, Tarek Rasouli, Nathalie Rasouli, Charlie Irrgang, Kris Kurowski, Sabrina Rill, Xaver Altmann, Lars Wich . . . and all the Rasoulution team

Then there's the list of amazing sponsors that have helped me throughout my career: Hope Tech, Lezyne, Five Ten, Red Bull, POC, Continental, Magura, GoPro (especially all the crew who helped on *Cascadia*), Evoc, Spank, Muc-Off, Tarty Bikes, Inspired Bicycles, Santa Cruz Bicycles, Lizard

Skins. And finally, Matt Allen, for his patience and hard work in helping me put together this book, and all at Penguin Random House.

Keep on riding!

Danny